THE
Wizard of Oz
AND
OTHER Narcissists

THE
Wizard of Oz
AND
OTHER Narcissists

Coping with the One-Way Relationship
in Work, Love, and Family

Eleanor D. Payson, M.S.W.

Julian
Day
Publications
Royal Oak, Michigan

The stories and vignettes in this book are composite and fiction-alized sketches to protect the anonymity of any particular individual. The ideas in this book are based on the author's clinical experience with the dynamics of narcissism in individu-als and groups and as such are not intended as a substitute for psychotherapy or other professional services. The reader should consult a qualified mental health care professional or other com-petent professionals in the event that any particular symptoms may require diagnosis, therapy, or medical attention. The check-lists in this book are not designed to substitute for professional evaluations or psychotherapy.

For information about seminars, presentations, or professional consultations, go to: www.eleanorpayson.com

Cover Art: Chris Dodge

First printing 2002
Second printing 2003
Third printing 2004
Fourth printing 2007

ISBN 978-0-9720728-3-0
LCCN 2002106815

DEDICATION

This book is dedicated to the loving memory of my father, mother, and brother. I also dedicate this book to my loving husband and son for their unfailing support and endless encouragement to bring my dream to fruition. And to God's grace and the inseparable nature of truth and love.

TABLE OF CONTENTS

FOREWORD

When Ellie first approached me to write the Foreword to this book, I was deeply honored. I have known her for over a decade; first as a respected colleague and then as a beloved friend. Our bond was immediate and our connection strong—even from the onset. Although we shared many similarities, the powerful force that drew us was our experiences with people in our lives who were characterized by Narcissistic Personality Disorders (NPDs). Not that we initially discussed this—but the results of such encounters made us sensitive and empathetic to one another. We recognized and mirrored certain realities in our respective beings.

Over time, numerous discussions about NPD evolved and flourished. Of course, I had studied NPD in my formal training; however, Ellie's knowledge, wisdom, and insight on the topic, as well as her ability to communicate it, was enlightening and empowering—beyond anything I had encountered. It made this often-neglected area of mental health and emotional healing easy to grasp and apply.

For that reason I remained a staunch supporter of Ellie throughout the writing of this book. I knew how very fortunate you, the reader, would be in having this book come to fruition. So, consider this book a gift from a talented therapist and wonderful human being as you pursue your personal journey towards healing and wholeness.

Harriet Haberman, Ph.D.
Leonia, New Jersey
April 19, 2001

ACKNOWLEDGMENTS

The journey in writing this book has been as wonderful, terrifying, and challenging as the story of Dorothy and her friends, and like Dorothy, I have been blessed with many remarkable and generous people along the way. The inception of this book began twenty years ago with a client I will simply call J. and her own courageous struggle to understand the profound way that she had been impacted by a narcissistic parent and spouse. Her determination lit the flame of my own desire to make more tools available on the subject of narcissism. I wish to express my gratitude to J. and the courageous efforts of many clients whose willingness to share their stories has enabled me to crystallize some of the central issues involved in coping with and healing from the impact of narcissistic individuals.

Each friend and colleague who encouraged, supported, and guided me had something special and unique to offer as my commitment to write this book unfolded. To my inspirational friend, Jeannie Ballew, M.A., who threw down the gauntlet, I want to express my profound appreciation for challenging and assisting me to develop the outline for the book and continuing to hold the vision from beginning to end. My deep gratitude to the nurturing friends who listened to my endless chatter about narcissism, read my manuscript, and surrounded me with the echoes of mothering love; Catherine Bartley, Debbie Holzen, Carol Rondello, Veronica Maher, M.S.W., Carolyn Daitch, Ph.D., Mary Anne Lushe, M.S.W., Julie Garvey, M.S.W., Marcia Bonahoom, M.S.W., Marianna Manion, Ph.D., Donna Manczak, Ph.D., Carole Kirby, M.S.W., John Hribljan, M.S.W., Ken Meisel, M.S.W., Julia Beard, M.S.W., Sue Ellen Eisenberg, Esquire. In acknowledgment for helping me on the last leg of this journey, many thanks to Larry Ferstenfeld and

Julie Greenberg, Esquire. I also thank Harville Hendrix, Ph.D., and the entire Imago therapy community with special gratitude to Margaret Mason, M.A., and the late Randall Mason, Ph.D., for leading a wonderful Imago therapy study group and sharing their wisdom regarding issues of narcissistic wounding.

Many thanks to the coaching of Bob Davies, M.A., and the editing help of Margie Summerscales, M.A., without whom the journey would have been a dry desert indeed. To Rebecca Ensign, I wish to express my appreciation for her final phase editing. And to Chris Dodge for his wonderful cover art, and Cathy Bowman for her help with the cover and interior book design.

Additionally, I want to thank the women and men who contribute so generously to the ADDA (Adults with Attention Deficit Disorder Association) world, who have unstintingly supported the dreams and goals of every person who comes to the table, especially Arthur Robin, Ph.D., Terry Matlen, M.S.W., and Wilma Fellman, M.A. I greatly thank my colleague, mentor, and friend, Sari Solden, M.S., for her generous support and constant confidence in my ability to bring this book to completion.

Finally, I wish to express appreciation and gratitude to my devoted friends, Harriet Haberman, Ph.D., and Sally Palaian, Ph.D.; my appreciation to Sally for her loving energy, commitment as a peer coach, and indispensable "body double" contribution in the writing process; and to Harriet for her loving generosity of spirit, her support on the long road of this project, and her belief in me.

My greatest appreciation goes to my husband, Tom Janes, for his many years of support and generosity of time in helping me hone the final version of this book.

INTRODUCTION

For countless generations, the average person has been encountering and coping with individuals who suffer from character disorders—one of the most significant, yet least understood, of these character disorders is the narcissistic personality disorder (NPD). However, there have been few tools available for the layperson who finds himself confounded by the difficult realities of being in a relationship with the NPD individual—whether it is in a work, love, family, or friendship relationship. The relentless need for the narcissistic individual to command the majority of another person's resources will eventually deplete the energies of the healthiest individual.

In addition, the NPD person's complete self-absorption results in an insidious tendency to devalue those within his or her sphere of influence, either subtly with condescension, or openly with criticism. The inevitable impact on the individual in a relationship with an NPD person is a dangerous erosion of self-esteem.

As a therapist in private practice, I have often helped people struggling to deal with the myriad and confusing array of defenses in the NPD person. This book is meant to be a map for the person who wishes to return from the world of Oz, where all roads appear to be going one way—in the direction of the narcissist.

I also hope that this book will stimulate a larger discussion about healthy versus unhealthy narcissism, eventually leading to a greater degree of psychological understanding about each other and ourselves. I have tried to write this book in an easy-to-read handbook style that includes vignettes, visuals, and metaphors that reflect the deeper realities of narcissistic wounding. Also, for the sake of ease in reading, I occasionally use "NPD" as an abbreviated reference to the NPD individual.

· Because women allow themselves the assistance of therapy more than men, I have unfortunately had fewer opportunities to work with men who find themselves caught in these types of relationships. However, the research shows, with a 60/40 ratio of men to women, that women are almost as likely as men to manifest the narcissistic personality disorder. Consequently, we are on safe ground regarding this disorder as an equal opportunity problem and can acknowledge that men do indeed struggle in these relationships almost as often as women do. Therefore, I have written this for both men and women. In pursuit of this goal, I have alternated gender pronouns throughout the book when referring to the NPD individual.

The stories and vignettes are composite and fictionalized sketches to protect the anonymity of any particular individual. Again, I sincerely thank the many men and women who have courageously committed to their own healing and allowed me the privilege of assisting them on their journey.

The Story of Narcissus

In Greek mythology, Narcissus was the handsome youthful son of the river god, Cephissus. His beauty was so captivating that he became the object of love and adoration of many women, but he rejected their advances. Among the love-struck maidens, was the nymph, Echo, who, as a result of displeasing Hera, the goddess of marriage, was condemned to a life of silent thoughts and feelings; all she was able to do was echo back what was said to her.

Therefore, upon falling in love with Narcissus, Echo was unable to tell him. She could only watch and worship him at a distance. One day, as Narcissus was walking in the woods, he became separated from his companions. When he shouted, "Is anyone here?" Echo joyfully answered, "Here, here." Unable to see her hidden among the trees, Narcissus cried, "Come!"

"Come, come," replied Echo as she stepped out from the trees that had shielded her. With outstretched arms, Echo rushed toward Narcissus. But he refused to accept her love. She was so humiliated that she hid in a cave and, over time, disintegrated, until nothing was left of her but her voice.

To punish Narcissus, Nemesis, the avenging goddess, made Narcissus fall hopelessly in love with himself and his own beautiful face. He spent the remainder of his life gazing in admiration at his image reflected in a pool. Unable to remove himself from his own reflection, he laid on the ground at the edge of the water until he gradually pined away. At the place where his body had lain, a beautiful flower grew—it was named, Narcissus.

CHAPTER ONE

Somewhere Over the Rainbow

The Illusory World of the Narcissist

Imagine a therapy session with a mother, her 16-year-old son, and a therapist. The son's grades are dramatically declining, and he is in danger of being cut from the basketball team. The therapist asks, "So, David, this possible set back doesn't seem very real for you. Tell me what losses you have experienced so far in your life?" The mother interrupts, "I know. Remember when I wasn't selected for the team fundraising committee?" David, facing away from his mother, raises an eyebrow and rolls his eyes as if to say, "See what I mean?"

This vignette captures the dilemma that occurs when you are in a relationship with someone who has a narcissistic personality disorder (NPD). Like David, just when you think it's your turn for attention the narcissist takes cuts. Somehow you are never included in the picture with the narcissist, and you may find yourself wondering: "Who am I if I am not allowed to exist?"

The word narcissism in its most fundamental sense means a tendency to self-worship. For the narcissist, his excessive self-absorption is a protection against unconscious but powerful feelings of inadequacy. Seduced by the narcissist's camouflage of outer charm or confidence, you are eventually drawn into the nightmare side of this relationship. By the time you realize that something is wrong, the cumulative effects can range from bruised self-esteem to severe depression.

The more days, months, or years you have invested in a relationship with an NPD person, the more difficulty you will have recognizing that you are on a one-way street, with all the attention, support, and recognition going the other way—his way! Your confusion and self-doubt are important warning signals that you may be encountering someone who has a narcissistic personality disorder. The purpose of this book is to provide some basic tools for understanding and dealing with the emotional impact of these relationships. You will also learn how to protect yourself from the frequent assaults to your own sense of self.

Let's look through the zoom lens at a social encounter with what I call the "overt" NPD person. From a distance, this individual appears rather intriguing, charming, and even charismatic. With a closer look, however, you notice that she is monopolizing the conversation and appears animated and engaging as long as the focus is on her. After further observation, you notice this warmth and animation quickly evaporate as you inject your thoughts, experiences, or feelings into the conversation. As the focus returns to her, she is re-energized and engages your attention with a certain gravitational pull.

You are increasingly fascinated with her performance and even more so as she selects you to be her exclusive audience. Perhaps some uneasiness sneaks into your consciousness, and you wonder about the need to get back to your schedule for the day, or you may wonder if you are up to matching her charisma, intelligence, or energy. At the same time, you sense that she needs your appreciation. You realize that you are in the presence of someone with great pride, and you don't dare yawn, glance away, or look at your watch. After ending the conversation, you may sigh with relief as if to say, "Whew! Now back to planet earth and the business at hand." Or perhaps you think, "Wow, *that* person is amazing!" You may sense a touch of admiring envy but also relief that you don't have to stay in the commanding atmosphere of her presence. Chances are you have taken a spin on the dance floor with the "overt" NPD individual.

Now, let's look through the lens from the other side at the "covert" or sometimes termed "closet" NPD individual. For example, perhaps you decide to visit a colleague's spouse, a physician who is an acknowledged expert in treating your illness. On your first appointment, he impresses you with his interest, professionalism, and expertise. He seems sensitive to your needs yet clearly in charge of the situation. You are compelled to be the good patient because you already feel privileged to have his special treatment and attention. You invest significant time and effort going through the tests he has ordered, and he is now recommending treatment.

The problem for you, however, is that the treatment is fairly extreme, with certain risks involved. As you muster the courage to ask him questions, he becomes defensive and tense. When you suggest that you want to give yourself time to consider this treatment option, he becomes cold and detached. He brutally informs you that, unless you follow his treatment, your symptoms will worsen and your prognosis is hopeless. Furthermore, he lets you know that he will not continue as your physician unless you comply with his recommendations. With an icy demeanor, he escorts you out the door. The shock and disbelief you feel are only a temporary numbing of the hurt, confusion, and outrage to follow. You have probably had a close encounter with the "covert" NPD individual.

This example reveals how devastating it can be to invest effort, time, and trust into these relationships. Regardless of the narcissist's public persona, the outcome is the same. Eventually, you lose. One reason for this is that the general rules of reciprocity are not working with the NPD person. The relationship begins to operate more and more on his terms, as if these are the only terms.

The seduction into the narcissist's world is profound. Even when you recognize the dynamics, you must work to resist the narcissist's manipulations. In fact, therapists with expertise in this arena know that it is unwise to treat more than two or three NPD individuals at any one time because of the enormous amount of energy and attention they require.

The severity and intensity of this disorder comes from the NPD individual's desperate pursuit to gain a *sense of self.* He consciously understands none of this, yet his inner need to feel worthwhile causes him to manipulate people in order to maintain an endless supply of attention, control, status, money, power, or recognition. This single-minded purpose covers the almost malignant anxiety and emptiness he feels.

Totally unaware of his inner problems, he looks to the world for fulfillment, relentlessly driving himself and others to meet his grandiose expectations.

The difficulty recognizing this problem early in your relationship with him is due to the fact that the deeper issues of narcissism can exist behind many different personas. A covert type of NPD person may appear shy, with a quiet authority. You, therefore, assume this individual has a quality of humility and expect that he will be sensitive to your feelings. If he is an overt type of NPD person, you may notice a more obvious attempt at dominating you, but the seduction of his charm may camouflage these behaviors. Distracted by his presentation, you let go of your ability to recognize his limitations.

One helpful approach to identify whether or not the person you are involved with has a narcissistic personality disorder is to reflect on your own feelings. So, as a start, I offer you a list of questions that will assist you in detecting this problem in a particular relationship.

1. Do you frequently feel as if you exist to listen to or admire his or her special talents and sensitivities?

2. Do you frequently feel hurt or annoyed that you do not get your turn and, if you do, the interest and quality of attention is significantly less than the kind of attention you give?

3. Do you sense an intense degree of pride in this person or feel reluctant to offer your opinions when you know they will differ from his or hers?

4. Do you often feel that the quality of your whole interaction will depend upon the kind of mood he or she is in?

5. Do you feel controlled by this person?

6. Are you afraid of upsetting him or her for fear of being cut off or retaliated against?

7. Do you have difficulty saying no?

8. Are you exhausted from the kind of energy drain or worry that this relationship causes you?

9. Have you begun to feel lonely in the relationship?

10. Do you often wonder where you stand in the relationship?

11. Are you in constant doubt about what's real?

12. Are you reluctant to let go of this relationship due to a strong sense of protectiveness?

13. Are you staying in the relationship because of your investment of time and energy?

14. Do you stay because you say to yourself the devil you know is better than the devil you don't know?

You may notice that the painful struggles reflected in these questions reveal what are often called codependent behaviors. Generally, these are behaviors that are care taking of others to the point where you and your needs are lost. While the NPD individual invariably attracts those who are vulnerable to these types of behavior patterns, the truth is that almost anyone will be pulled into care taking behaviors when interacting with the NPD person.

The impact on the codependent in a relationship with the NPD person is much like Dorothy's journey through Oz. As Dorothy believes that the Wizard is the only one who can help her, she tries harder and harder to please him. Similarly, your involvement with the NPD individual is characterized by an ever-increasing effort to please and gain approval. However, like the Wizard, the narcissist's approval is rarely given. Instead, you are more likely to see the unpredictable anger and rage over the smallest infraction or mistake. Great sensitivity to criticism, or intolerance of anything perceived as less than a perfect performance, can cause the NPD individual to unleash an outburst of sharp and hurtful rage. At times these experiences leave you feeling helpless, unable to do anything but crawl off to a corner to figure out what happened.

Over time, these behaviors insidiously lower your self-esteem and set you on a path of consistent and increasing self-doubt. The sheer intensity of the narcissist causes you to wonder what transgressions you committed to provoke such an outpouring of anger, disdain, or criticism. Sometimes a cold, unmoving stare from him communicates a chilling absence of all human feeling and a reflexive desire to run for cover. As your self-esteem withers and your confidence in knowing your reality diminishes, you gradually concede more power and control to the NPD person.

For all these reasons, you are in dire need of recognizing the nature of the relationship to regain a sense of self-esteem and equal rights. The devastating emotional impact of these relationships has many common features. For this reason, chapters four through seven are devoted to discussing the variety of patterns that exist, depending on the type of relationship: the parent/child relationship, the love relationship, and the professional or social relationship.

Let's return to our earlier definition of narcissism. In a general sense, narcissism means unrestrained self-love. By now, most of us have been exposed to the concept of our need for a healthy self-love in order to thrive, pursue goals, and find fulfillment in life. A parade of books helps us learn how to overcome the various ways that we suffer from low self-esteem, or a lack of self-love. Very little attention, however, has been paid to unhealthy or pathologic narcissism, which is found at the other end of the spectrum—self-love that is destructive.

Unhealthy narcissism is occurring when an individual excessively pursues admiration, attention, status, understanding, support, money, power, control, or perfection in some form. It also means that the NPD person is not able to recognize, other than superficially, the feelings and needs of others. The rules of reciprocity are not operating in the relationship. This is not to say that NPD individuals don't often shower others with attention, gifts, or favors. Indeed, they often do. But the ultimate goal is always for some kind of return. The giving may be to foster a certain image or an overall feeling of indebtedness in you, such as an IOU note to be called in at some other time. You, of course, would rather believe you received the gift because you are cared for and valued.

We all have some of what may be termed narcissistic needs such as the need to be valued, admired, understood, or simply recognized as a unique person. During painful periods, we become much more narcissistic, or self-centered, and our demands for attention, mirroring, validation, etc., increase. However, when we feel better, we generally return to a baseline ability to reciprocate in our relationships. Instead of only taking, we give-and-take by listening, understanding, validating, and supporting others.

For NPD individuals, however, they feel endlessly entitled to special consideration and attention. The narcissist somehow never moves past the unique circumstance that requires you to put yourself aside and realize that what's happening for him is *more* special, *more* upsetting, or *more* wonderful. Eventually, you realize that you and your needs are on indefinite hold.

The following examples depict some common scenarios seen in these relationships. Family members sigh and roll their eyes when, once again, the NPD dad changes the family's plans at the last minute to make sure that his needs and wants are the center of concern. Perhaps the NPD mother has yet again bluntly insulted her son's new date. Expert at distracting her, family members look around nervously and quickly change the subject to avoid taking mom on. These encounters and reactions are almost second nature and are rarely noticed unless higher stakes are involved.

When you are involved with an NPD person, you may continue to tell yourself that things will eventually even out—that you will get your turn, and when the time does come, he or she will be there for you, too. Yet, as you tell yourself these things, you continue to ignore all the clues. Then an event in your life focuses the spotlight on you, and you are shocked and disappointed by her behavior. For instance, your NPD mother sits sullenly in a corner at your wedding and pouts because *she* is not getting special attention. Or your son's NPD piano teacher goes into a rage when your son receives some temporary instruction from a resident concert performer.

Even more devastating, you discover that your spouse is incapable of showing empathy and support when a significant loss touches your life. These are just a few examples of the wake-up calls that can break the cycle of denial. At this point, you are finally ready to look at the destructive impact this type of relationship has had on your life, and you begin to consider your need to do something about it.

These crises are the watershed events that allow you to grasp the full measure of the NPD person's limitations. The moment of truth is often a confusing mixture of intense feelings. You might feel outrage, hurt, and betrayal. At the same time, you may feel released from the self-doubt that has dominated your thoughts and emotions. You no longer wonder if this person is off base, or if you are overreacting. You no longer wonder whether this person will reciprocate or change. You are finally released from this illusion!

At the same time, you may also feel a profound sense of loss, similar to a death. In many ways, the grief and sadness are virtually the same. In this case, however, it is the *wished-for* relationship that has died. This event can be the most powerful turning point in your life, especially if it involves an NPD parent or a spouse of many years. During these crises, you will want to seek support, possibly therapy, so that you do not miss the opportunity for healing and growth.

Many of the following chapters will explore in detail the healing process for the various types of NPD relationships. This process involves three distinct phases: awareness, emotional healing, and empowerment. Yet, regardless of the type of relationship, the process is always one of reclaiming yourself.

Dorothy's journey through Oz is a remarkable metaphor for the seduction into the narcissist's illusory world and the healing process that ultimately must occur. Dorothy believes that the Wizard is the only one who has the power to help her, and she embarks on one elaborate adventure after another to find favor and win his approval. Yet, the moment she sees past the larger-than-life image of Oz to the vulnerable little man behind the curtain, she begins to claim her own inner resources and power.

You too must see past the illusion of grandeur or special needs of the NPD person and understand the forces at work that keep you stuck, bewildered, frustrated, and ultimately used. This journey is inevitable for anyone who has experienced a relationship with a narcissist. The moment of truth is always painful but also presents the opportunity for healing to begin. Like Dorothy, you must discover this choice for yourself.

CHAPTER ONE SUMMARY

The overall definition of someone with a narcissistic personality disorder is characterized by a combination of severe limitations in understanding other people and their feelings, as well as an excessive pursuit of what are called narcissistic supplies, such as admiration, attention, status, understanding, support, money, power, control, or perfection in some form. While all of us need these supplies in adequate amounts to feel a sense of well being, the narcissist pursues them with an unrelenting desperation and a keen ability to manipulate others. Meanwhile the outer persona of the NPD individual is generally one of confidence and control, alongside a smooth or charming demeanor. As your involvement with the narcissist develops you will notice that the relationship increasingly becomes one-way with you in the primary giving position.

The common feelings that will begin to emerge for you are frustration, confusion, fear of confrontation, exhaustion, uncertainty of where you stand with him or her, inadequacy, neglect, disempowerment, loneliness, or alienation from family and friends.

We discussed how the narcissist attracts individuals who have vulnerabilities towards codependency or care-taking behaviors and offered a list of questions that can help you identify the warning signs that are reflective of a narcissistic dynamic in a relationship. The codependent dynamics of focusing on the feelings and needs of others, with an inability to identify your own wants and needs, become greatly exacerbated when involved with a narcissistic individual. Eventually, as the codependent, you have greater difficulty validating your own perceptions of reality.

The source of the narcissistic disorder is connected to a *deep unconscious experience of self as inadequate or flawed* for the NPD individual. The NPD person's desperate pursuit to gain a sense of self causes him to drive himself and others to meet his grandiose expectations. In general, there are two basic narcissistic personality types—the *overt NPD* and the *covert NPD*. Numerous personas are manifested within these two types.

Finally, we discussed briefly the three phases of healing from an NPD relationship.

Awareness: Recognizing the inability of the NPD to provide emotional support and a true give-and-take-in the relationship.

Emotional healing: Identifying, validating, and empathizing with your own feelings of wounding that result from the relationship with the NPD.

Empowerment: Identifying healthy versus unhealthy boundaries and assertively negotiating your own needs in the relationship with the NPD. This will lead to your awareness of the choices that are right for you regarding the relationship.

CHAPTER TWO

Seeing the Emerald Forest for the Emerald Trees

The Overt and Covert Narcissist

Some of the most difficult disorders for the layperson and psychology professional to understand are those that are termed character disorders, a category which includes the narcissistic personality disorder. The primary reason this disorder is so elusive to identify and complex to understand is that the NPD individual is often extraordinarily capable of maintaining an impression of competence and, sometimes, social charm as well.

In the public and social arenas, the NPD person often appears charming or perhaps reserved but always self-confident and in control. This outer image is projected with such consistency because it is motivated by the NPD person's *unconscious and all consuming drive to feel good enough.* In other words, the NPD person is often completely unaware of having significant problems. Only those who are closest to the NPD individual will be aware of a disturbance beneath the surface.

The NPD person's success in maintaining this illusion of competence and control to the outside world is perhaps the greatest source of pain for you if you are in a relationship with the narcissist. Whether you are the son, daughter, spouse, friend, or coworker, the underlying difficulties of the relationship are generally never seen by anyone else. This, in turn, causes you to continually doubt yourself since you rarely receive outside validation of what you are going through. Even mental health professionals can miss the boat in recognizing what you are up

15

against in this relationship. Without validation of your experience with the NPD individual, the erosion to your self-esteem becomes even greater.

In addition to living in such an isolated world with the NPD person, you are also exposed to endless criticism, controlling behavior, and unrealistic demands. On those rare occasions when others might observe some of these behaviors, they will often dismiss the incident with an automatic desire to make excuses for the NPD person. Caught up in the desire to believe in the NPD person's presentation, family and friends will avoid conflict by minimizing her inappropriate behavior, even at times siding with her. Although not conscious, everyone senses the potent sensitivity or volatility under the surface in the NPD individual.

For all these reasons, the nightmare side of these relationships is usually a private one, a nightmare that can only be stopped by receiving outside validation from a credible person who can offer a counterweight to the blame and criticism you are experiencing in the relationship. The NPD person's ability to project his problems onto you is so powerful, you have come to believe that you are the one with the problem. By now, with your self-esteem in full retreat, you probably feel angry, guilty, self-doubting, and simultaneously sorry for the NPD person. With such a confusing array of feelings you may doubt your own sanity.

In general, what you probably *are* experiencing might be termed neurotic issues. While many people react to the word "neurotic" negatively, in truth, it simply identifies a psychological state that almost everyone has experienced. Believe it or not, most people have struggled with neurotic issues at one time or another. As a professor said in a lecture I once attended, *"To be neurotic is a developmental achievement— not a developmental failure!"* In developmental terms, this means you have successfully completed the first three stages of life (attachment, exploration, and identity) with an overall intact sense of self.

The awareness of your feelings of fear, guilt, anger, sadness, etc. about some difficulty reveals that you have the capacity to observe yourself and recognize that you have a problem. This awareness also means that you will be more likely to seek some form of help to deal with it. Your concern and desire to take responsibility to work on yourself is the determining factor that identifies your successful passage through the first three developmental stages. In a nutshell, you are functioning at a significantly higher level when you have the capacity to reflect on your feelings and behaviors as well as the feelings and behaviors of others.

By contrast, the individual with a character disorder lacks the ability to recognize that he has a problem and, if confronted with this possibility, would not consider himself responsible in the matter. Essentially, the only difficulties or pain the NPD person will be conscious of are those negative consequences that his behaviors bring about, especially in his relationships. Regardless of his culpability, the NPD person will blame everyone else or the circumstances of his life rather than acknowledge that he has a significant problem.

A person who has psychological pain and is able to self-reflect will generally recognize that he is responsible to work on himself. On the other hand, the character-disordered person is unable to see his problems and expects others to take responsibility instead. *Consequently, the deep and severe disturbance of an NPD person is primarily seen in the pain he or she inflicts on others.*

Perhaps the situation becomes more clear if we say it this way: the character-disordered person is so disturbed that he is unable to see that he has a problem, while the individual with a particular neurosis is overall healthier, but unable to recognize her strengths. Therefore, the individual with neurotic issues needs help to identify her strengths and capabilities so that she can move on and enjoy her life.

So, don't become alarmed if you see aspects of yourself in these chapters. While you may have some psychological difficulties, you also have the capacity to recognize and be concerned about them. This is a psychological strength—not a weakness! It may also be distressing to realize that adults who have one or more narcissistic parents often share some of the narcissistic traits of their parents. However, the capacity for observing yourself and working on these characteristics is the critical distinction between having narcissistic traits and the full-blown disorder.

In my private practice, I am quite familiar with the tendency for self-reflective individuals to see themselves in a multitude of psychological descriptions and quickly become alarmed. The simple fact that you may be concerned about having some of these problems is a genuine indicator that you have an overall healthy sense of self.

As mentioned in chapter one, narcissistic traits are shared by virtually everyone to some degree because having narcissistic needs is normal, such as needing to feel valued and special for who we are, unique and individual. Narcissistic needs, therefore, include the drive to feel validated, admired, appreciated, valued, and loved. The healthy or unhealthy degree of narcissistic needs and connecting problems in a person could be depicted on a continuum that might look like the following:

Continuum of healthy-neurotic-character disorder

Healthy Self	Neurotic	Character-disorder
● Strong sense of self.	● Overall intact sense of self.	● Severely impaired sense of self.
● Capacity to self-reflect, acknowledge problems, and take responsibility.	● Ability to self-reflect, experience the pain of these problems, and have motivation for change.	● Little or no capacity to observe self and acknowledge problems.
● Defenses are flexible.	● Defenses at times rigid.	● Defenses rigid and brittle.
● Full capacity to empathize with others.	● Significant capacity to empathize with others.	● Little or only superficial ability to empathize with others.
● Narcissistic needs in balance with awareness of others and *their* needs.	● Narcissistic issues connected to specific emotional problems.	● Narcissistic issues connected to primary means of experiencing self.
● Conscience fully developed.	● Conscience developed with areas of distortion.	● Conscience not fully developed or at times marginally developed.
● Self-esteem is sturdy and resilient to the ups and downs of life.	● Low self-esteem issues are common; becomes fragile when encountering difficulties connected to emotional wounds.	● Self-esteem is merged with grandiosity and combined with defenses of "splitting" off parts of the unwanted self.

As you can see, *the significant dividing line between the neurotic and the character-disordered person has to do with the capacity of the individual for self-observation as well as for real empathy of others, which is integrally tied to the development of conscience.* Along the continuum are varying degrees of rigidity in the defenses, difficulty with self-esteem, and regulation of feelings and impulses. Even a person without neurotic problems will have times in her life when self-esteem suffers and narcissistic needs become greater.

To expand the continuum *within* the narcissistic personality disordered category, you will also see differing degrees of the NPD person's capacity to recognize his or her inappropriate behavior and acknowledge the harm done. The most important difference in degree of functioning within the character disorder range relates to the capacity to know and be concerned about values of right and wrong. A higher functioning NPD individual will have a rigid sense of right and wrong, which tends to be black and white, or concrete. She will often be extremely judgmental of others and harsh in her opinion of the necessary punishments for wrongdoing. While she may rarely apply these same standards of punishment to herself, she will, however, be concerned about following her standards of right and wrong.

The lower functioning NPD individual (in closer proximity to the sociopath on the continuum) will be prone to constantly bending the rules for himself although outwardly he may criticize others for a similar infraction or transgression. Alongside his tendency to disobey the rules, he will have no real remorse for the effects of his offenses on others and will rationalize his deceptive manipulations in any number of ways. The degree to which deceptive, harmful, and unlawful behaviors (termed sociopathic behaviors) are present in an NPD individual is of utmost importance if you are in a significant relationship. You will want to pay attention to the potential for danger to your own safety, whether it is physical, psychological, or financial.

The psychological mechanism of conscience in the lower functioning NPD person may be considerably less developed than in the higher functioning NPD person. At the same time, his periodic feelings of rage and inadequacy cause him to feel entitled and justified in his actions. An example of an individual at this level of functioning would be a man who has been a respected judge, perhaps known for his tough handling of criminals. Then, one day you are shocked to read in the papers that this judge has been leading a double life—taking bribes and engaging in multiple illicit affairs. In fact, this scenario happens all too often when we learn about the other side of a public figure thought to be beyond reproach. Although this is an extreme example of the more severe and sinister type of NPD individual, the narcissist is never the person he appears to be in the public sphere.

The NPD individual is generally entirely unconscious of his disturbance. All avenues of experiencing self are dependent on successfully acquiring control, praise, admiration, special consideration, power, status, etc. Externally, the person appears confident and in control while the interior life is one of constant self-critiquing against the illusive standards of greater success and control. The result is often a desperate discontent and, at times, an overall feeling of deep inner unhappiness. This interior life may outwardly resemble a constantly shifting pattern of moodiness. In addition, any disruption in the maintenance of these rigid standards can result in intensely expressed anger or self-pity. The brittle defenses, which protect the NPD person from feeling the inner wound to his unconscious experience of self, cause him to be exquisitely sensitive to the slightest possibility of criticism, being overlooked, or having his wishes dismissed.

For the sake of providing you with the most current mainstream criteria that psychiatrists use in making the diagnosis of NPD, the *Diagnostic and Statistical Manual of Mental Disorders, Fourth Edition, (DSM IV)* states:

DSM IV—criteria for diagnosing the narcissistic personality disorder

"A pervasive pattern of grandiosity (in fantasy or behavior), need for admiration, and lack of empathy, beginning by early adulthood and present in a variety of contexts, as indicated by five (or more) of the following:

1. has a grandiose sense of self-importance (e.g., exaggerates achievements and talents, expects to be recognized as superior without commensurate achievements)

2. is preoccupied with fantasies of unlimited success, power, brilliance, beauty, or ideal love

3. believes that he or she is "special" and unique and can only be understood by, or should associate with, other special or high status people (or institutions)

4. requires excessive admiration

5. has a sense of entitlement, i.e., unreasonable expectations of especially favorable treatment or automatic compliance with his or her expectations

6. is interpersonally exploitative, i.e., takes advantage of others to achieve his or her own ends

7. lacks empathy: is unwilling to recognize or identify with the feelings and needs of others

8. is often envious of others or believes that others are envious of him or her

9. shows arrogant, haughty behaviors or attitudes."

Another trait that was included in the *DSM III*, prior to 1994, is one that I will mention here, "reacts to criticism with feelings of rage, shame, or humiliation (even if not expressed)."

Overall, you can see that the NPD person displays a formidable set of traits that reveal a tremendous conscious belief that he is special, unique, and deserving of everything that a person of such special status should have. This acute sensitivity to criticism or being overlooked is often the only outward evidence of his feelings of inadequacy and experience of self as "*flawed*" or "*shameful.*" Because of his difficulty receiving criticism, as well as his inability to empathize with another person's feelings, the NPD person usually finds it impossible to admit wrongdoing, express remorse, or apologize. Other traits commonly seen in the NPD individual are a tendency towards compulsive behavior, anorexia, bulimia, perfectionism, addictions (often cocaine), suspiciousness, hypochondria, aggression, and deceit. Above all is the NPD person's need for control, particularly in close relationships.

While a ponderous debate takes place in the psychology field as to whether or not the narcissistic personality disorder is a set of early and profoundly developed defenses, the result of a separate line of development, or even a deficiency in the developing brain, the debate will not be resolved here. However, we must begin to understand the profound limitation that the narcissist has in comprehending the reality of a person other than himself.

Imagine for a moment that you do not experience yourself as a "self." From this perspective, you can understand the difficulty the NPD person has in recognizing the unique and separate existence of another "self," or person. In a sense, the narcissist views others and the world around him as an extension of himself, perhaps as you might view your arm or leg. Because the narcissist can only understand others by absorbing them into his own experience of self, he determines that others should behave and act the way that HE behaves and acts. Again, to use the analogy of the arm and leg, he unconsciously expects you to conform to his will, just as his own arm or leg would do. When your behavior deviates from his expectations, he often becomes as upset with you as he would be if his arm or leg were no longer under his control.

However, the narcissist has learned that other people do not always do his bidding or meet his demands in the way that he expects. He has, therefore, developed formidable manipulation skills, at times deceitful, to achieve his goals. Sometimes these skills are a highly developed ability to charm and bring others under his spell or influence. Other times he may be exceptionally good at utilizing intimidation, power plays, or intellectual prowess. Yet another style is the martyr manipulation of using helplessness, obligation, or guilt. In many ways, the narcissist has assessed, with considerable skill, the vulnerabilities of another person. He then effectively manipulates this person until he achieves his desired outcome. These dynamics of power will be discussed in greater depth in chapter three.

For now we will simply highlight the understanding that, above all, the narcissist feels obliged to continually let people know how they should be doing things and to correct their actions at almost every turn. This behavior may only be revealed in his closest relationships, such as with his spouse and children. He has an almost self-righteous attitude that this is his mission in life, as if he were captain on a ship of fools. Since his own internal relentless drive for perfection, control, or some special status is never really satisfied, he cannot acknowledge you for a job well done. His inability to recognize your achievements is due to the unconscious but deeply felt experience of inadequacy. Consciously he is only aware of his envy of you and your success. Unless he can take credit himself for your achievement, he is unlikely to validate it as successful.

An exception to this pattern of withholding praise may occur when the NPD person chooses an individual or one of his children whom he feels reflects back the admiration and success of his special standing. These chosen few may be lavished with attention and appear as if they can do no wrong. Even these individuals, however, are subject to the tyranny of the NPD person's control and are held hostage to his will for fear of losing the rewards that go with this special standing.

One of the most striking and painful experiences in the relationship with the narcissist is her inability to empathize. Again, if we remind ourselves that the narcissist's understanding of another person's reality is limited by seeing this person as an extension of herself, we can begin to see why she is incapable of empathizing with another person's feelings. For instance, imagine an NPD mother feeling upbeat and good when her daughter comes home from school. If her daughter enters the house feeling down, her mother may admonish her for her feelings or cajole her to feel better. She is unable to acknowledge that her daughter's feelings are different from hers and that she has good reasons of her own for her feelings. On another day when her daughter comes home in a good mood or excited about some positive event, and her mother is angry or down, she will inevitably criticize or punish her child subtly in some way for not reflecting back the same mood that she is experiencing.

The NPD person's inability to empathize, which is the capacity to be aware of and care about another person's feelings, is also the reason that she can at times verbally shred you. Empathy, like the brakes on a car, provides the ability to maintain control of our anger. For the narcissist, however, once the rage is tapped, you may feel like you are standing in front of a fire hose as he verbally attacks or physically intimidates you. Although rarely expressed, these experiences prompt a gut level awareness in you that he is unable to recognize your basic human rights of respect and consideration. At this point, the narcissist is having a meltdown to the unconscious feelings of *self as inadequate* and the surrounding feelings of rage.

In this context, I am not talking of the often ugly, but fairly normal, dirty fight that might break out between partners or family members who are capable of empathy. Instead, I am referring to an extraordinarily intense verbal attack that knows no bounds. It may even be delivered with a calm, icy quality that in some eerie way is divorced from all human emotion, where only the mechanistic goal to annihilate is experienced. Whether it is an explosive hot rage or an icy calm attack, the narcissist's anger is an unmistakably different experience from the anger expressed between two people who are capable of empathy.

In the aftermath of the NPD person's meltdown, he will often feel an extreme resentment towards you for causing him to lose control. He may even shut you out for a period of time, refusing to speak about the incident again. These are dramatic experiences that demonstrate how the NPD individual is unable to recognize the impact of his behaviors and acknowledge his own problems. In addition, these episodes are devastating for you as you realize he is unable to empathize with your feelings.

Perhaps a more common style of dealing with anger for the NPD person is to completely ignore you with a dismissive and indifferent demeanor. However, this coping style of suppressing and covering anger will also lead to the rare but extremely intense rages previously mentioned.

The martyr response is another way the NPD person can punish you and express anger. The NPD person who manifests the martyr persona (perhaps more common to the female narcissistic persona) is continually using guilt and self-pity to instill a sense of obligation that you should conform to her wishes. When you assert your own desires or differences, she will generally increase these behaviors, displaying an angry, quiet misery as she denies herself any pleasurable involvement with you. If she feels strongly enough, she may, with great drama, enlist the sympathy of others to join her in a chorus of scorn directed at you, *the offender*. She may then shun you for an indefinite time period until she is satisfied with your show of repentance and apology.

Finally, you may encounter the NPD individual who appears to never express anger. He may comply or cheerfully agree with you on the surface and, once out of your sight, go about doing exactly as he pleases. When you attempt to confront this behavior, you are met with an endless variety of smoke screens consisting of forgetfulness, rationalizations, blame, or simply playing dumb as to how such a misunderstanding occurred. If you confront the issue, you will likely be met with the stonewall defense of his refusal to talk about it. On rare occasions, you may trigger the rage that is always at the core. However, this defensive pattern in an NPD person rarely allows such a display of anger.

Another exasperating occurrence in close relationships with the narcissist is her inability to give. Whether it is money or any act of giving, *the narcissist can rarely give anything freely, or give in ways that will truly make you happy.* Unconsciously, her envy and pain make it impossible to enable you to be happy. Equally evident is her inability to share in your joy if you should have good fortune or success. Since the NPD person must always feel "one up" with you "one down," acknowledging your success would threaten her defensive need to feel superior.

You will remember that the narcissist's need for attention, power, etc., are primary avenues of experiencing himself as a self. Therefore, *money is frequently experienced as a "self-object," meaning that it has for all practical purposes the significance of being as important to him as his arm or leg.* Just as you would no more give up your arm to someone, so too the narcissist cannot give his money, even to those closest to him. If something is given, strings or conditions are generally attached although this may not be explicit at the time. Children of NPD parents instinctively understand this from an early age in their relationship with the parent and look for alternative routes for getting what they want, at times developing keen abilities for outmaneuvering the NPD parent. Many of these dynamics, which have unique variations, will be explored further in later chapters dealing with the different types of relationships with the NPD person.

For the moment, let's return to the surface image the NPD person projects in his social and public sphere. An interesting twist on the picture of the narcissist is the fact that these traits will be more easily seen, to some degree, depending on whether or not the persona is an overt type or a covert type. Whatever self-image the NPD person has chosen, it is usually fixed and rigid and the focus of excessive, perhaps total, self-absorption.

The overt type of NPD person is someone whose self-image or identity allows the more open expression of narcissistic needs such as admiration, power, control, etc. This individual may be a powerbroker using his skills in public endeavors, perhaps as a high achieving executive, politician, diva, daredevil, sports figure, or even revolutionary. In the public arena, the overt narcissist gains attention through a larger than life display of charm, intimidation or other grandiose reflections of high status, money, etc. Whatever the self-image is, the overt type of NPD person uses his persona to directly take the spotlight and openly demand an endless supply of public attention such as admiration, respect, awe, or perhaps even fear.

Socially, the overt NPD type is apt to convey the feeling that you are the audience, there to enjoy her entertaining personality, to be impressed by her power, money, intellectual prowess, or physical prowess. You might feel drawn into her sphere, as if you were being swept into a trance. You may also have a feeling of intoxication as this happens because the NPD individual is conveying the message that you too are special, so special that she wants to charm you.

After more consistent contact, you will notice the consistency of this pattern, and you may be gaining your first clue of the narcissistic dynamic. In a deeper relationship, the NPD individual will exhaust you in his need for your constant attention and appreciative support, yet his desire to charm you will insidiously give way to sarcasm and competitive tension.

One of the myths commonly believed regarding the narcissist is that he does not have many friends. Quite the opposite is true of the overt narcissist, who often surrounds himself with a busy social life. These relationships are, in fact, a carefully selected group of others who either share similar traits or are content to participate in a supporting role. While these friendships may appear long standing or significant, they are generally superficial and require minimal emotional investment on the part of the narcissist.

Unlike the overt narcissist, the covert or "closet" type of NPD person gains admiration, status, and control through more subtle and indirect means. His demeanor is typically more reserved and self-contained, at times aloof. The covert NPD person will display a persona that allows him to cover and disguise the grandiose needs by displaying an identity of helper, humanitarian, expert professional, rebel without a cause, misunderstood artist, or hermit. This persona allows the narcissist to gain attention, status, and power through *what he is doing and what he is connected to*, rather than attempt to command a truly solo role in the spotlight. In fact, the covert narcissist may at times outwardly show a disdain of the spotlight with an aloof and indifferent demeanor.

The covert narcissist may manifest his persona in a role that is identified as humanitarian such as the doctor, therapist, minister, or missionary. In this circumstance the narcissistic needs for attention are acquired through the role, as the NPD individual harbors the grandiose fantasies inwardly that he is one of the "chosen" people, doing good work for the betterment of humanity. The narcissistic grandiosity in this circumstance is manifested in a self-righteous pride and a feeling of self-importance that has little to do with the person's genuine ability for empathizing with the feelings and needs of others. At times this NPD individual may not possess a strong personality, yet is completely invested in maintaining the illusion of selflessness while gaining his need for status and attention through the persona of his larger than life cause. Only in the privacy of this NPD person's relationships with the required "give and take" of empathy and support will you evidence the painful limitations and defenses of his narcissism. Similarly, his expression of anger is also generally covert with the dynamics of an insidious passive aggressive pattern.

The identity of the self-sacrificing mother or father is another example of the covert narcissist. Here the NPD parent will strive endlessly on behalf of her child and gain the need for attention and admiration through a martyr-like expectation of undying loyalty and appreciation alongside frequent reproaches to her child for not showing enough gratitude. This narcissistic parent also tends to hold up impossible standards (subtly at times) and simultaneously communicates relentless messages of the child's incompetence to meet these standards. Like the covert NPD individual, she lacks the ability to empathize, and disguises the narcissistic needs for attention with a demeanor of constant fretting, worry, and overprotection.

Another NPD persona can be one of "becoming," such as the artist who never paints or the inventor who never invents, yet believes himself to be in the process of greatness. The presentation is one of becoming but somehow never quite arriving. Finally, an extreme example of a possible covert NPD type might be the identity of the misunderstood hermit or loner. This identity may cover the individual's grandiose fantasies that he is so great that no one else is capable of appreciating how special he is. Therefore, the entitlement, grandiosity, contempt, and envy of others exist only in his deeply hidden fantasy life.

Similar to the overt NPD type, the covert NPD person will reveal the same narcissistic traits in a relationship as it deepens. These surface descriptions do not characterize anything significant by themselves. Only when the individual reveals the underlying characteristics of the narcissistic personality disorder does it become apparent how the persona serves to meet the extreme narcissistic needs. In other words, the basic dynamics of the disorder are identical in both types. Only the public persona varies.

As with any generality, exceptions always exist and you may find various combinations of these traits in the NPD individual. Overall, issues of narcissism exist on a continuum, and you may see these same personas to a lesser degree in individuals who have narcissistic traits, without the underlying narcissistic disorder.

Regardless of the outer persona, as you become more deeply involved with the NPD person, you will notice that the relationship begins to immediately place you in the primary giving position. You are probably also rationalizing your support because of the special qualities or special needs of the NPD person. Meanwhile, you may be reassuring yourself that things will balance out in the end.

Your first real evidence of the degree of unhealthy narcissism will most likely occur when you either decline a request or assert a need of your own. Because of the NPD individual's need for power, control, and special consideration, he has already been securing these things in the relationship. By the time you wake up to this fact, you may find it extraordinarily difficult to readjust the thermostat.

Although the overall picture of the NPD person's capacity for change may appear discouraging, growth and change are sometimes possible. As with any disorder or illness, distinct conditions and behaviors exist that will increase the chances of motivating the NPD individual towards change. Regardless of the ability for deeper change on his or her part, you can still reshape the relationship to one that is more tolerable and perhaps enjoyable for you. Your capacity to recognize the powerful dynamics of the NPD person and to hold your own in the labyrinth of his defenses is the first step towards healing and empowering yourself in these relationships.

Neurological Considerations

There are a number of organic disease processes that can contribute to a physiologically induced form of narcissism. Illnesses that affect the central nervous system, such as multiple sclerosis, certain cancers, different forms of dementia, even aggressive chemotherapy treatment, and others can all contribute to changes in the brain that cause the individual's personality to mimic the NPD of extreme self-absorption and a loss of the normal range of emotions. These manifestations of narcissism can virtually replicate all the dynamics that we are discussing throughout this book.

Your recognition of the organic basis for an individual's narcissism can allow you to modify your expectations, grieve the loss of the person you once knew, and employ the same strategies of setting limits on inappropriate behaviors. In this scenario your understanding of the individual's impairment can help you maintain a compassionate stance while recognizing that you must take over the functioning of a more mature adult. Your own self-care is inevitably a priority if you are going to "go the distance" as a caretaker for your loved one. There may be support groups and other resources that are invaluable as you cope with the significant stresses and losses involved in this painful deterioration process.

With advances taking place every day in our understanding of the brain, we may eventually see connections between neurological deficiencies and the personality disorder of narcissism. In fact, there is provocative research underway that reveals possible neurological impairment due to problems in the bonding phase of childhood. Some researchers in this area suggest that the interference with the child's ability to regulate his/her emotions impairs the normal process of the child's developing brain creating a physiological basis for the impairment for empathy.

At present, the best we can do is treat the side effects and byproducts of the NPD—the most common being depression, obsessive-compulsive behaviors, and vulnerability to addictions of all kinds. These comorbid, or additional problems that exist alongside the NPD can exacerbate and at times masquerade as the narcissistic personality disorder, and once treated, may allow the individual a healthier ability to relate to others and the world.

Among other neurological illnesses that exacerbate narcissistic tendencies are extreme forms of attention deficit hyperactivity disorder, Tourette's syndrome, and Asperger's syndrome. When these problems are identified and treated, the remaining issues with narcissism may be significantly softened. Consequently, accurate diagnosis and treatment of the comorbid problems can significantly enhance the outlook for change.

CHAPTER TWO SUMMARY

In this chapter we discussed the primary characteristics of the narcissistic personality disorder and some of the difficulties of being in relationship with him or her. The most painful reality for those in relationship with the NPD person is not having outside validation for the problems beneath the surface. Other people may have a tendency to primarily see the larger than life persona of the NPD. This inability for others to recognize the deeper realities of the NPD individual is due to the narcissist's capacity to maintain a consistent, self-confident, and smooth demeanor to the outside world. This insidious alienation and isolation intensifies your issues with codependency and causes a severe lowering of self-esteem.

We also discussed the key characteristics of the narcissistic personality disorder.

Limited or no ability to:
- Self-reflect and take ownership of a problem
- Tolerate anything perceived as a criticism, oversight, or dismissal
- Recognize others as separate selves—free agents with free will
- Feel genuine empathy for others
- Recognize the needs of others
- Negotiate anger—periodic loss of control of anger, outbursts of rage
- Acknowledge or praise other people's accomplishments—due to envy
- Genuinely apologize or feel remorse

Excessively:
- Requires attention, admiration, special consideration, or recognition
- Demonstrates a grandiose sense of *entitlement—a hallmark!*
- Controls and manipulates others to achieve his/her goals—tenacious and persuasive
- Criticizes self and others
- Holds unrealistic expectations of self and others

- Holds an over-estimation of self and his/her needs—maintains the belief that he or she is more unique and special than others—grandiose self-image
- Manifests compulsive behaviors
- Demonstrates an all or nothing approach to life
- Compulsively pursues status, power, money, beauty, recognition, etc.

As individuals all of us fall somewhere on the continuum of narcissistic traits and have normal needs for the *narcissistic supplies* of recognition, empathy, appreciation, and support. In addition, when under stress, we have a tendency to require more comfort, attention, and support from others than we are perhaps able to give. However, when the stressful period passes, a person with an overall healthy sense of self will return to the balanced give and take of reciprocal sharing with others. The narcissist, however, rarely moves past his or her excessive need for the narcissistic supplies and maintains an unrelenting tendency to feel that his needs and/or circumstances are more special, more unique, or more important than yours.

We also discussed the continuum for the higher versus lower functioning NPD person primarily characterized by the degree of conscience and concern for right and wrong behavior. At the heart, a sense of conscience is based on the ability to recognize that the rights (feelings, needs, freedom) of others are equal to those of our own. For the NPD individual, this recognition is impaired in differing degrees of severity, at times combining unlawful (sociopathic) behaviors, which can involve significant danger to your own safety in a relationship.

Finally, the contrasting personas of overt and covert narcissism in the NPD individual were outlined.

The overt type gains narcissistic supplies through charm and a public persona that allows for the grandiose displays of high status, money, and power.

The covert type gains narcissistic supplies of admiration, status, and control through his or her role connected to a larger than life cause.

The different personas in the overt NPD such as powerbroker, diva, stage mother/father, etc., or the covert NPD such as humanitarian, "righteous ideologue," expert professional, etc., are descriptive types merely meant to demonstrate the variety of surface manifestations that can be seen in the NPD person. These profiles only reflect the narcissistic personality disorder when they are accompanied by the deeper characteristics we have discussed.

The most *important first step* towards healing and growth for you as a potential codependent in relationship with the NPD person is to validate your perceptions of healthy versus unhealthy sharing and to recognize the deeper picture of the narcissistic disorder when present in a person.

Follow Your
Yellow Brick Road

The Boundaries of Self

By now, you have gathered that the narcissist's behaviors manifest themselves around a desire for power and control. While the first step to healing and empowering yourself is to recognize the presence of the narcissistic disorder, you must also understand how and why the NPD person is so effective at establishing power and influence. Recognizing these dynamics will help you to "hold your own" in these relationships. Ultimately, you will discover the capacities for healing and change on the part of the NPD person as well as determining what you want and need from this relationship.

Consider that the NPD person is on a constant mission to achieve a sense of "self," driven by his obsessive desire for a particular set of ideal standards. These standards are, in turn, defined by his self-image and he seeks them with the fervor of his whole being. Therefore, *your experience with the NPD person will be determined in large part by how he sees you supporting or not supporting his unconscious agenda for self.*

Initially, the NPD individual will assess whether or not you are deserving of simple recognition because you either promote or threaten his experience of self. If he perceives that you neither enhance nor threaten this pursuit, you will most likely be dismissed or perhaps not acknowledged at all. For instance, in a line at the grocery store, the mother of your child's schoolmate may appear utterly indifferent that her child is chatting away with yours despite the fact that you have seen each other many times at the school they both attend. In this scenario, you are merely inconsequential to the NPD individual. Therefore, you don't exist for her! While it may be insulting and annoying to receive this kind of treatment, you can see how the narcissist creates a narrow and impoverished world for herself as she attempts to censor and eliminate all experiences irrelevant to her standards.

You may remember that the narcissist essentially experiences and understands others as if they were an extension of his own *self*. He, therefore, feels entitled to what you have to offer without concern for true reciprocal exchange on his part. This inability to recognize the boundary of *you* as a free agent with your own ideas, feelings, and desires, along with his intensely felt sense of entitlement, are the powerful forces at work behind the scenes in virtually every interaction. *The most insidious and subtle dynamic underlying all interactions with the NPD individual is his unconscious capacity to turn his lack of boundaries into an asset by causing you to lose the boundaries that define you.* In this context I am using the word "boundary" to indicate the recognition that you are a separate person with your own needs, rights, preferences, and ability to make your own decisions. The most common result of being in a relationship with the narcissist is that sooner or later you find yourself orbiting within his sphere of influence, having lost sight of your own feelings, opinions, preferences, and goals.

If the NPD individual has decided that you are a person worth pursuing, he will attempt to draw you into his arena, inspiring you and causing you to lose track of your own agenda and priorities. While all of us can use behaviors to manipulate others for our own gain, the NPD individual is compulsively driven to come out ahead in relationships and employs a number of strategies in this pursuit. The behaviors that accomplish this outcome have a variety of forms but generally fall into one of the following nine types: Admiration/Idealization; Martyr/Guilt; Intimidation; Distraction; Devaluing; Repetitive Criticism; Double Message/Double Bind; Projection; and Emotional Hostage.

Each of these dynamics includes many unconscious defenses and conscious behaviors designed to protect the narcissist from experiencing his own sense of inadequacy. These behaviors also support his imperative to feel "larger than life." As we identify these patterns of interaction, you will understand how they inevitably render you increasingly unable to take care of your own needs and interests in the relationship.

Depending on the nature of your involvement with the NPD individual, he will automatically begin sizing you up for his estimate of your value to play a part in his pursuit of *self*. If this is a business relationship and he has decided that you are a source of competition (or he sees you as a threat for any number of reasons), he may attempt to neutralize your power by intimidating and devaluing you in the presence of influential people. If he has decided that you are a *significant* threat, you will immediately begin experiencing behaviors designed to devalue you in one way or another. He may be overt about this or extremely deceptive and covert. In the latter case, you would not be given any external clue that he has decided to wage war against you.

However, because the NPD individual is so entirely unconscious of his own grandiosity, you will generally gain a hint of his agenda as he reveals an attitude of contempt towards you either subtly or openly. If you can identify the NPD individual early in the relationship and tune in to the potential for sabotage, you can set up boundaries for safety or increase your sources of accountability to validate your performance and contributions in a given situation.

The Admiration/Idealization Dynamic

Generally, the NPD person will not be threatened enough in the beginning of a relationship to immediately craft warfare. Far more common is the approach of "absorbing you or your abilities," and this could potentially occur through a combination of strategies. A more overt NPD person will shower you with her charm and charismatic display of humor, drama, or wit. With such a captivating performance, you may feel disoriented, off balance, and unsure of what's going on. You may also feel completely enamored with her personality and apparent confidence. In these situations you invariably feel a sense of intoxication that you are being courted in this way.

The power of the NPD person to bring you into unconscious agreement with her belief that she is someone truly extraordinary is possibly the most remarkable feature of the narcissist. Before you know what's happening,

you may be following her lead, enjoying the charisma, or perhaps in-
timidated by her persuasiveness, power, and authority. You may not
realize that you are losing track of your agenda and, at the same time,
deferring to hers.

The narcissist's belief that you, too, are special because he has selected you to associate with him is the other compelling force at work.
In fact, who isn't vulnerable to the warming glow of admiration, especially from someone with such apparent personal power? If we add that
you also admire him for his accomplishments, or that he is able to facilitate your goals, the charm of the NPD person may indeed be
irresistible!

In the circumstance of mutual admiration or an exciting shared
goal, you can maintain an observing eye on the potential for the narcissistic dynamic. You will learn to maintain conscious awareness of the
intoxication of mutual positive regard due to the fact that it becomes
both an idealization and distraction dynamic causing you to forgo your
desires and lose your ability for self-care. Perhaps nothing inspires us to
forget our agenda more easily than the temptation of infatuation, which
tends to induce a sense of feeling larger than life. Basking in the glow of
mutual admiration with the narcissist, we may easily gain an inflated
sense of ourselves.

Behind the scenes of this heady experience is the insidious condi-
tional expectation of the narcissist. As he lavishes you with his attention,
opportunities for special status, or financial enhancement, he also induces you into a sense of obligation and disproportionate loyalty. His
expectations for the return on his investment will eventually be clear.
Setting limits on his unrealistic expectations will be greatly influenced
by your ability to keep track of your boundaries in the relationship.

*At the beginning of a romantic relationship, the NPD individual is
often the pursuer with an ardent intent to capture you—the idealized perfect partner.* Whether the pursuit is subtle or direct, the NPD individual
will not rest until he secures his goals for the relationship. You may
literally be swept off your feet by his adoration and intensity. This initial phase of the relationship, which is characterized by the NPD person's
idealization of you, will be followed by a subtle or not so subtle "turning of the tables" once the relationship is secured. The NPD person's

increasing dissatisfaction with you just as you are risking significant emotional investment can be painful and baffling. You may find yourself asking, "What happened to the love we shared? How could he claim to love me so deeply and be so cruel?" Your concern and uneasiness around questions like these are important signals that alert you to the potential of a serious narcissistic dynamic in the person you love. We will return to the unique features of the love relationship in chapter six.

The Intimidation Dynamic

The intimidation dynamic can also draw you into conciliatory and deferring behaviors. The NPD individual's capacity to intimidate is something he has generally developed into an art. Intimidation is not only an overt power play. You may also feel a subtle air of authority, an aloof sense of scrutiny, and an indifferent attitude towards you. Depending on your need to have this relationship go well, you may or may not be bothered by his aloof demeanor. But when your own desires are at stake, you may find yourself drawn to "make an impression" to find out where you stand.

Perhaps you are consciously drawn to the challenge of establishing some sort of rapport. Meanwhile, the NPD individual may respond only to your admiration and support causing you to invest more energy in these behaviors. On other occasions, you have no idea where you stand, and you become uneasy as you receive no real feedback or response from the NPD person. This style of interaction is more often the pattern of the covert narcissist who draws you into a perception of how exceptional he is through an aloof and indifferent manner. Only as he feels you are offering the proper appreciation will he allow you a closer association. His behavior reinforces your need to pursue him, thereby increasing your motivation to please him and go out of your way to win his approval. The shifting dynamic of pursuer and pursued is already in progress and will intensify until the relationship is progressively on the NPD person's terms.

At other times, the intimidation dynamic may be more overt, such as when the NPD person directly wields his authority by making continual references to the differences in your positions of power, professional stature, status, or money. In this scenario, you may feel obligated to keep a low profile in an attempt to establish some sense of harmony. Unfortunately, at the same time, you may also be giving up opportunities to express your opinions and assert your needs. On the other hand, if you confront the grandiose competitive display head on, you will usually discover the NPD person's readiness to define the lines for competition and invite the devaluing behaviors or covert manipulations.

Although you may feel daunted by the challenge of dealing with these issues and wish that the difficulties of this relationship would somehow just go away, you inevitably pay a higher price later if you ignore the problems. You can often level the playing field in these relationships by developing and using assertiveness skills and setting boundaries early in the relationship. These skills must be mentally and emotionally rehearsed, preferably with the help of an outside support person or therapist. You will want to anticipate and prepare yourself for the narcissist's defensive behaviors that may arise as you employ your new skills. We will explore the various empowerment strategies in depth when we look at the different types of relationships with the NPD individual. For the moment, let's return to the range of behavior patterns you may observe in the initial phases of the relationship with the narcissist.

The Martyr/Guilt Dilemma

Another primary dynamic of power is the martyr role, generally seen in the female narcissist. Often subtle at first, you will be drawn into the NPD individual's world through her display of unique or special suffering. Her flattering, self-effacing invitation for you to help her accomplish a task or engage in an activity can be the lead-in for you to listen endlessly to her dramatic and seemingly catastrophic problem(s). Meanwhile, she may simultaneously communicate how special you are with your exceptional abilities to listen, provide hope, and give assistance. Only after considerable repeat contact do you realize that her circumstances are forever dramatically urgent, and you are now in the unenviable position of being her irreplaceable support person. As you attempt to backpedal out of your support role, the martyr behaviors intensify with sullen and hurt expressions of recrimination from the NPD individual.

Your own sensitivity or unwillingness to hurt her feelings will certainly play a role in keeping you hostage to these manipulations. If you are already in the position of primary care giver, the entanglement can be formidable and difficult to extract yourself from. You may need to enlist outside support and develop self-care abilities that help you value your time and energy with effective boundary setting.

Consequently, you are better off allowing your support role to develop slowly until you know how much energy and time you can afford. Proceeding slowly will also surface the expectations on the part of the NPD person giving you a chance to make a course correction before you commit yourself.

The Distraction Dynamic

Another manipulative behavior on the part of the narcissist is a continuous ingenuity for creating a sense of distraction. While distraction can be positive or negative, you may notice an ongoing ability for the NPD person to defocus you or those around you from the intended agenda. For instance, just when a board of directors might be ready to discuss the implementation of an agreed plan, the NPD person raises a new issue and the subject at hand stalls out. This power to distract may be facilitated through humor, shifting the topic, making catastrophic predictions, subtly pitting individuals against one another, creating an atmosphere of distrust, or simply asserting a last minute change of mind, etc. Meanwhile, the NPD person is jockeying for position for the moment when he can take over the program and gain control. *The more chaos and confusion that exists in any given situation, the more possibility the narcissist has to wrest power and assert his goals.* Again, you can see the pattern of blurring boundaries as the narcissist distracts you from your own intentions in the relationship.

Distraction dynamics are often a defensive reaction on the part of the NPD person to avoid an issue that he or she would rather not address. Defocusing the subject by bringing up a counter complaint is probably the most common form of distraction. If you are not prepared and ready to stay calm and firmly stand your ground, you will quickly be pulled into the escalation of action-reaction. Anne Katherine's marvelously clear book, *Where to Draw the Line,* is a helpful resource with lots of examples of boundary errors and violations and the variety of assertiveness skills that are needed to hold your own.

For the NPD person, the most common distraction is to immediately bring the subject back to herself and change the focus to a different issue. The "broken record" technique is particularly effective when encountering the distraction dynamic. This skill requires your ability to remain calm and keep a fairly neutral tone as you simply restate the same message, altering the phrasing but not the message. Each time the NPD defocuses the issue onto herself, you can respond, "I am aware that you may have an issue of your own, but we are not discussing that right now. You are not listening to what I am saying." Then repeat your message.

Or perhaps at a meeting, you state that you recognize the NPD person's issue but wish to return to the subject on the table and finish this first. *The primary skill you will learn is to calmly, but firmly, reclaim the focus and restate your message.* Only after rehearsal, along with trial and error practice, will you discover your strengths and weaknesses and improve your overall ability to use these skills.

At other times, when you are simply sharing your thoughts about a subject of interest, the NPD individual may begin sharing something so unrelated that you wonder if you fell down the rabbit hole in Alice's wonderland. In addition, humor that has a quality of absurdity is another form of distraction that often occurs to distance you, not allowing you the opportunity to share feelings about something you care about. Perhaps you feel dismissed, as the NPD person not so subtly reclaims the spotlight.

Depending on the importance of the discussion and the context, you will choose the level of assertiveness that you want to use. You may want to find an ally and/or distance yourself, perhaps cutting your visit short. Passive aggressive dynamics such as these are common when dealing with the NPD person and difficult to confront. These behaviors require an extra measure of practice and learning with assertiveness skills. We will return to some of these behavior patterns and self-care skills in chapters five through eight.

These various dynamics of power and manipulation can, of course, be expressed in any combination and in a variety of styles. Regardless of this, however, the underlying dynamics are always the same—the experience of being drawn into the NPD person's boundaries, while losing track of your own boundaries. If you have codependent tendencies, you may find that your impulses compel you to expose yourself all the more by offering support and becoming more vulnerable. You may tell yourself, "No problem, I can go the extra mile. I can show him that I trust, care, and like him." You may continue to invest in your relationship with the NPD individual in a misguided attempt to bring him around. At this point, you become a willing participant in your own boundary violation.

One of the most helpful tools you can begin to work with is to consciously recognize these dynamics and develop your own finesse and strength in maintaining the boundaries in the relationship. Your awareness of these behaviors will help you maintain your perspective and retain a sense of your thoughts, needs, and goals in the relationship. Keeping track of your desires and asserting your needs early in the relationship with an evaluative eye on the other person's reactions will help you discern the level of functioning you are encountering.

The more signals you receive that you are dealing with the narcissistic dynamic, the more you can consciously slow down the progress of the relationship and the depth of your involvement or investment. Slowing the pace of your developing relationship will help you to expose the realities of the narcissistic individual, since the NPD person cannot easily tolerate the give-and-take of mutual pace-setting. Having said this, however, *you may only discover the depth of the NPD issues once you have already risked significant involvement.* At this point you will be more vulnerable to his ability for wielding influence and power.

The Devaluing Dynamic

As you can already see, many of these dynamics overlap and the distraction behaviors of the NPD person often involve subtle devaluing messages. However, sometimes you may experience a devaluing dynamic immediately. For instance, perhaps you are being introduced to a group of mothers at school. As your friend introduces you to another mother, she suddenly stops the conversation to question you, "So, your last name is Wilson and your husband's name is Strom. Doesn't your son find that confusing?" Perhaps she even continues to lecture you in front of everyone about how confusing and hurtful she thinks this is for your child. Situations like these are also termed passive aggressive because, although this mother is devaluing you in front of a group of women, you are not in a situation where you can truly confront her. In addition, the power of being stung in a public situation generally renders most of us unable to think effectively, not to mention manage our emotional reaction.

Consequently—*when in doubt or on the spot—give yourself permission to take time and/or space!* Keep several neutral phrases in your hip pocket for these occasions such as, "You have an interesting perspective. I'll have to think about that," (take time) or "I'm not sure this is the place to discuss personal choices," (take space). Both of these interventions allow you to reclaim your personal boundary and regroup.

When the NPD individual repeatedly violates your boundary, perhaps by calling you "honey" when you have asked to be called by your name, *you can use an intervention called therapeutic bewilderment.* In this case, you throw the responsibility back to the NPD individual by asking in a calm tone, "I'm confused about why you are still calling me honey when I have asked you several times to call me Jennifer. Can you help me understand this?" While this certainly confronts the NPD person, you are allowing him to grapple with a boundary violation with some time and space of his own.

Generally, respectful assertiveness interventions are very effective and allow you to keep your interactions with the NPD individual from becoming one-sided too quickly. In addition, asserting your limits immediately in the relationship commands respect, a character quality that must be fought for with the NPD person. Practice and patience with yourself is important as you learn how to develop these self-care behaviors.

So far we have talked about the various dynamics of power that you may experience with the NPD individual in the initial phase of the relationship. And, of course, you are better off identifying these issues early so that you can assess how worthwhile it is for you to continue the relationship. However, if it is a family relationship or one that has already developed into a significant involvement, that is, a business relationship, friendship, or romantic relationship, you will undoubtedly have already begun to experience the devaluing dynamics of the NPD person.

As your investment in the relationship intensifies, you will begin to receive more and more messages that the NPD person sees you as deficient in some way. At this point the NPD person is projecting his unconscious feelings of self as "shameful" or "flawed" onto you. He is increasingly finding fault or dissatisfaction with you and also expecting you to defer more of your time, attention, and preferences to him. If you are in an intimate relationship, you may find yourself struggling to recapture the excitement and euphoria of the early relationship. You are also no doubt beginning to go through a process of intense self-evaluation, wondering if the NPD person's criticisms of you are valid or if you are causing this painful deterioration.

Once you enter the inner sanctum of the NPD person's world, you are now subject to the dark and unconscious side of the narcissist's experience of self. When you invariably frustrate his exquisite sensitivity to appreciation and admiration, or disappoint his expectation of you as his perfect ideal, he will project his anger and rage and will demonstrate a variety of defensive behaviors to keep you in line. He may periodically point out a "laundry list" of reasons why you are not measuring up. He may simultaneously compare you to his ideal standard and communicate his disdain with your incompetence. Implicit in these interactions is the baffling and confusing dynamic of the "double message" or "double bind."

The Double Message/Double Bind Dynamic

A double message consists of two messages delivered simultaneously that are in direct opposition to one another. The narcissist's conscious and unconscious experience of self is the embodiment of the double message. For example, unconsciously she experiences herself as inherently flawed and shameful; however, consciously she experiences herself as superior and upholding standards of perfection that few others can achieve. Therefore, her projection of this contradictory reality would be communicated in the themes of "You must be perfect," contrasted with the message, "You are so incompetent; you can never do it right!"

An example of this communication is illustrated in the following vignette of an NPD mother who has always valued education and admired individuals who have achieved high levels of academic success. When her daughter, who has achieved advanced degrees, finally confronts her mother about her lack of acknowledgment for this, her mother replies, "Well, I never understood why you wanted to work so hard." Her mother's response not only fails to validate her daughter's desire for acknowledgment, but also reveals her mother's opposite message—that education is not a worthy enough pursuit and is perhaps a waste of time! This is an apt example of the contradictory messages you can receive from the narcissist. No matter which message you respond to, you receive the devaluing message from the opposite side.

Perhaps the message is something like an NPD parent telling his son, "You can do anything you want to if you try," while simultaneously finding endless fault or reasons why one goal after another is not realistic or not a good idea. Another example would be for the NPD partner to admonish her partner for not expressing how he really feels; when he does express his own thoughts, she finds endless fault with them or becomes outraged that he would have such thoughts.

As one client of mine put it in a session, "This stuff is crazy making!" And, indeed, the double message does trigger confusion and self-doubt because it sets in motion a no-win situation. Regardless of the message you choose, the trap snaps shut with the consequence of feeling devalued. Eventually, when you receive unremitting double messages, you will begin to doubt your sanity, and self-esteem will wither. The only way out of this labyrinth is to identify the subtle (and sometimes unspoken) contradictory messages in the confusing array of criticisms and confront this reality openly.

For example, a client we will call Laura decided that she simply could not tolerate listening to her mother's relentless complaints about her physical health. Beyond her mother's endless ventilation was the fact that Laura's response didn't matter. Whether she empathized or tried to assist in problem-solving a matter, her mother would only intensify her expressions of self-pity and remain unreceptive to any attempts on Laura's part to reassure her or to assist her with problem solving.

After some mental and emotional rehearsal in therapy, Laura eventually asserted her frustrations to her mother. First, Laura calmly described the behaviors she observed in their interactions and then gently but firmly let her mother know that when she ventilated like this in the future, Laura would not be willing to listen beyond five minutes. Laura's eastern European mother resisted Laura's assertions and said that she couldn't stop and wouldn't stop because ventilating made her feel better. Laura responded by acknowledging her mother's feelings and then reiterated her message, asserting again that she could not tolerate the frustration of listening endlessly to her mother's physical complaints. At this point her mother angrily countered in Polish, "Well, every man for himself!" Stunned, but not surprised, Laura later repeated the phrase to her father, to make sure she had understood the translation of her mother's words. Indeed, she had. Her mother's emphatic retort had revealed the naked truth of her narcissism—if your needs and my needs are in conflict, it's every man for himself!

While this was far from the last time that Laura would assert her intention to change the pattern of her interactions with her mother, her mother did begin to respect Laura's position and alter her behaviors in the presence of her daughter. The initial steps for Laura, however, required her ability to identify and confront the double message, as well as communicate and demonstrate her unwillingness to be a participant. Finally, as Laura became more confident in her ability to assert her needs and follow through with her stated intentions, she recognized that her mother did indeed begin to change her behavior patterns and treat Laura with more respect in their relationship.

A poignant depiction of this problem can be seen in the movie *Shine*. *Shine* is essentially the true story of a sensitive, gifted young man and his narcissistically wounding father. Even though the father has devoted his life to the development of his son's music, he forbids his son from taking true ownership of his abilities and his life. The tragic outcome of such a double bind is for the son to go mad. In this miraculous true story, we are allowed to share in the journey back to selfhood for the adult son. In the end, he is able to reclaim his music as his own and recognize that his relationship with his father is beyond all hope. He may even continue to gain strength and relieve his symptoms as he faces his deeper feelings of rage and hurt surrounding the many painful moments of psychological abuse.

The Repetitive Criticism Dynamic

The narcissist generally has an endless repertoire for delivering criticism; by the time you are well into the relationship or have grown up in the relationship, defending yourself and your position has become a knee-jerk reaction. This pattern, however, only further undermines your self-esteem because you have already fallen into the trap of validating the criticism by defending yourself. Countering the criticism with an explanation or a rebuttal also serves to encourage the narcissist's desire to pursue his critique all the more because you are now fully in his arena, debating his issue in terms of *his* original premise. Unless you are prepared to take "his" course in logic and debate, you are better off walking away from the argument.

The following vignette offers an example of a woman who is learning to maintain an awareness of boundaries without getting drawn into a pattern of self-defense. A mother complains to her daughter that she just doesn't understand why her daughter buys an item of food and gives a list of reasons why the food is unhealthy. The daughter, who has begun to identify the dynamics of her mother's narcissism, calmly reasserts her own boundary by saying, "Mom, I bought that for me, not for you. You don't have to eat it." In this instance the daughter is able to firmly avoid the setup to argue the point about whether or not the item is worthwhile to eat and instead responds to the issue of boundaries, asserting her right to choose what she wants for herself.

In the same way, when you confront the double message, you empower yourself by resisting the urge to try to satisfy the NPD person. You will need experience and practice to detect the underlying contradictory messages. Once you recognize these messages, you can feel confident in your ability to "opt out" of the no-win situation.

You can also address the ever-present criticisms arising from the illusive and unrelenting standards of perfection as you begin to assert your refusal to tolerate these evaluations. Calling attention to these instances of unnecessary critique and letting the NPD person know that you will not accept these behaviors is another step towards reshaping the relationship to one that is healthier for you. You will need to repeatedly point out these occasions and be ready to provide consequences such as ending the discussion or leaving the room. *While the NPD individual may not understand the "whys" or "wherefores" of your changes, he is capable of learning which behaviors you will not tolerate and to refrain from those behaviors in your presence.* These changes will require your constant maintenance with periodic reminders—calling them to your parent's attention or reasserting consequences for using those behaviors.

Similar to Laura, a client we will call Theresa initiated a discussion with her NPD mother after considerable work and preparation in therapy. She had carefully practiced the basic strategies of assertiveness behavior with one important difference: her recognition of her mother's narcissism. This recognition allowed Theresa to be realistic about her expectations for change on the part of her mother, which included an awareness that her mother would be unable to acknowledge or grasp Theresa's feelings. In addition to this, she could anticipate her mother's defensive responses such as the attempt to distract Theresa and change the focus of discussion.

When it came time to initiate the discussion, Theresa was able to repeatedly refocus the discussion, no matter how much her mother attempted to grab the spotlight and turn the discussion into one about herself. Once Theresa communicated a clear and specific description of her mother's critical behaviors, she calmly expressed the hurt and angry feelings she had when these interactions occurred. Finally, she gently but firmly asserted her refusal to tolerate these behaviors and let her mother know that when she engaged in criticizing her, she would respond by ending their discussions.

You may realize from Theresa's scenario that these interventions take an emotional readiness that occurs after working through some of the confused, angry, and hurt feelings that exist due to these relationships. Preparing yourself requires mental and emotional rehearsal, which means rehearsing the assertive behaviors, as well as anticipating the defensive reactions and maneuvers on the part of the NPD individual. Last, but not least, is the importance of following through with the stated consequences when the narcissistic behaviors recur. A well-tested guideline for effective assertiveness skills is: don't begin the process until you are completely confident that you can follow through with your stated consequences. Otherwise, you end up further behind than when you started!

The Projection Dynamic

At the heart of the devaluing behaviors of the narcissist is the projection defense. The negative projections of the NPD person originate from his unconscious self-hate and rage due to his deeply felt experience of self as flawed or even nonexistent. Because the narcissist is so completely unconscious of this reality, he instead looks out at the world and others (especially those close to him) and sees them as inherently flawed or inadequate. He then feels compelled to let you know all about these flaws and may at times verbally attack you for any number of reasons. If the projection goes full circle, you will walk away feeling completely flattened, miserable, and confused, with your self-esteem dangerously close to subzero. When this happens, *the NPD person has successfully projected onto you his own experience of self and caused you to feel exactly how he feels inside (although unaware of these feelings).*

If you don't recognize what's going on in this dynamic, you will be vulnerable to believing his projections. In addition, you may find enough truth woven into the assault that you get lost examining and defending yourself. When you begin to fully appreciate the fact that these attacks are often unconscious projections on the part of the NPD person, you will be able to psychologically buffer yourself from the toxic impact of these messages. This will allow you to gain perspective as you evaluate your own contributions to the problem.

One of the most powerful abilities of the NPD person is the way he projects the illusion that his logic is airtight and his analysis well reasoned as he astutely points out your weaknesses and problems. Before you realize it, your back is to the wall trying to defend yourself against a barrage of mesmerizing attacks. These attacks may come in rapid fire, a calculated dissection of such intensity that you feel no choice but to burst out like the Incredible Hulk! As you reflect on your behavior later, you may shrink in shame at your loss of control and the terrible things you said. These episodes of your own loss of control only intensify your fear that you are, in fact, the one with the real problem.

The mental capacity of the NPD individual is often formidable, and his ability to appear cool and in control only reinforces the appearance of his superior capacity for "objective truth." Often, his tone of disdain or outrage is so convincing that you cannot pause to think, and the impact of his delivery is so effective that you do not even examine the premise or point that underlies such an attack. When you begin to recognize the maneuvers that distract you from your own thoughts and feelings, you can call a "time out." This will help you declare your right to discuss an issue with ground rules that allow each person to be heard in a safe and more respectful forum. While these assertive behaviors take practice and work, setting limits on the inappropriate escalation of conflict will go a long way toward improving your feelings of safety and self-worth.

The Emotional Hostage Dynamic

The final, most lethal condition of the relationship with the NPD individual is what I call the emotional hostage phase. By now the relationship has deteriorated to the point where minor issues become escalated arguments. Power plays with the NPD person wielding threats of all kinds are a regular pattern. Perhaps you also engage in the warfare with threats of your own. Your fear of the NPD individual's rage, along with your fear of his disregard or rejection, may paralyze you from acting on your behalf to get outside help.

At this point, your self-esteem is at an all-time low and you are probably questioning your own mental health. Your increasing starvation for some sign of love and acceptance from the NPD person is likewise contributing to your inability to act and make decisions that will benefit you. This phase is very much like the phenomena of "burnout" in a job that is increasingly draining your energy, rendering you unable to act and take steps for change. The path of least resistance is to keep treading water and hope that some improvement will occur. This holding pattern may also seem preferable to taking on the NPD person's defenses. No doubt you are reluctant to risk rocking the boat because you have invested so much of yourself—in years, emotional effort, or life decisions. The potential losses you face as you challenge the NPD person feel daunting.

In addition to the possible losses, you fear the NPD person's capacity for retaliation. By now you have had enough experience of the rage just below the surface to be fully aware of his potential to retaliate with all the tools of power at his disposal. Your fear of this rage is well founded and one of the best reasons why help from an outside professional can become so necessary. Along with this recommendation, I would add the cautionary note that a professional's opinion is certainly not a guarantee that you are receiving the best advice. Depending on the severity of your circumstances, you may want to secure the opinion of more than one professional. The important message here is that you start the process of seeking outside assistance from a person who can begin to give you the perspective you need.

We will discuss the importance of committing to the process of healing and change in subsequent chapters. You may already realize that simply getting out of a dysfunctional relationship is not the full answer, lest you turn around and repeat the pattern again—a scenario I have witnessed on far more than one occasion in my private practice.

Perhaps the most surprising but commonly shared fear is that your efforts to change your situation with the NPD individual will be the cause of his catastrophic self-destruction. You are not only aware of his capacity for rage but also his deep vulnerability. Even though you have never understood his problems, you have long sensed the presence of some deep wound. You can't imagine the guilt you would feel if your actions precipitate his deterioration. The dilemma for you has become a growing awareness that survival is coming down to him or you. Serious symptoms for you may range from depression to chronic anger to stress-related illnesses, or the use of escape mechanisms such as compulsive or addictive behaviors.

You may be adhering to the belief that the goodness of love and the passage of time will bring change and healing. Because this is not the forum to speak of the possibilities that come from faith intervention, I will simply say that the NPD person is unlikely to change without the proactive efforts of someone close to him. Much like the dynamics of the disease of alcoholism, the NPD individual needs to see the consequences of his narcissism and to recognize that he must face his behaviors, if not his inner issues, in order to continue his relationship with you.

If the relationship has developed to any of the painful realities just described, you need to confront your own denial and allow yourself to benefit from the assistance of a professional skilled in NPD issues: someone who can help you begin the journey of healing and the retrieval of your self-esteem. When you are ready, you will be able to use new strategies to discover the potential for change with the NPD person and, eventually, make the choices that you feel are right for you.

CHAPTER THREE SUMMARY

Because the NPD individual is unconsciously unable to experience a full sense of "self," he primarily experiences other people as an extension of himself. He therefore interrelates with others by absorbing them into his boundaries. The NPD person uses a variety of unconscious behaviors that influence you to lose the boundaries that define you.

The nine main types of manipulative behaviors that influence another person to lose track of his or her boundaries are: admiration/idealization, intimidation, distraction, martyr/guilt, devaluing, double message/double bind, repetitive criticism, projection, and emotional hostage.

Admiration/Idealization—A dynamic involving the NPD person's ability to draw you into a sense of awe and admiration for her unique qualities, abilities, status, power, etc., or to keep you at a distance until you are able to reflect back the proper level of appreciation that she expects. By contrast, if you have something she wants, she may court you with special attention, a seduction that often feels irresistible.

Martyr/Guilt—An ability of the NPD person to portray "special suffering" that enlists you as the "indispensable" caretaker and includes a subtle or overt reproach if you should let her down.

Distraction—The continual tendency for the NPD person to take the spotlight of discussion back to himself, or to defocus a conversation onto a subject that he feels will give him the upper hand.

Intimidation—The use of power in a subtle or overt display that induces you into conciliatory or deferring behaviors.

Devaluing—An effort to demean and diminish your thoughts, feelings, and abilities through subtle or overt criticism, alongside references that heighten his stature.

Repetitive Criticism—A cycle of dialogue that begins and ends with constant criticism of your opinions or choices when they depart from the NPD individual's reality.

Double Message/Double Bind—The dynamic of conveying contradictory messages on the part of the NPD person. Often subtle and difficult to recognize (such as verbally communicating one thing while non-verbally expressing another), you may only discover the "set-up" after you attempt to satisfy one of the messages. In this moment, you receive a critical or devaluing response from the NPD person for not adequately responding to the opposite message.

Projection—Rooted in the NPD person's unconscious sense of self-hate (self as inadequate), this perception becomes directed outward as the narcissist sees others as flawed instead. She then reacts to these flaws with a righteous zeal that fuels her critique and aggression towards others.

Emotional Hostage—The final phase of "victimization," evidenced when your self-esteem has waned to such a degree that you are dispirited, drained, and unable to validate your reality. The result of being subjected to this treatment is your inability to set limits, act on your own behalf, and ultimately make important decisions about the worthiness of your relationship with the NPD person.

The more serious dynamics of power and manipulation evolve as you enter the inner sanctum of the NPD person such as the intimate relationship, the parent/adult child relationship, or other close relationships involving interdependence. If you are in a relationship with the NPD person and experiencing these behaviors, you are likely having extreme difficulty sustaining a sense of self-esteem and confidence. You may also feel a pervasive self-doubt about your own perceptions of reality. Eventually you may become subject to the emotional hostage dynamic where you are unable to leave, yet also unable to act on your own behalf. Depending on the severity of your circumstances, you will need some form of outside assistance or professional help to stem the tide of your emotional burnout and begin the process of healing and change.

CHAPTER FOUR

A Horse of a
Different Color

The Parent/Child Relationship

The Old Lion and the Fox

A lion, enfeebled by age and no longer able to secure food for himself by hunting, determined to do so by cunning. Taking himself to a cave, he lay down inside and pretended to be sick. When the other animals came to call and inquire after his health, he sprang upon them and devoured them. Many lost their lives in this way, until one day a fox called at the edge of the cave. Suspecting trickery, the fox asked from a distance, how he was doing. The lion replied that he was not at all well. "But," he said, "why are you standing outside? Do come in."

"I would do so," said the fox, "but I see that all the footprints point toward the cave and none the other way!"

—Aesop's Fable

Old Lion in Aesop's fable is an uncanny analogy of the overall experience of the child and later the grown child of a narcissistic parent. With an inner wound that disables the narcissist, compassion and a deep longing compels the child to repeatedly strive for acceptance and love from the NPD parent. Yet, like the visiting animals in this fable, the painful conclusion is to be devoured by the unrelenting needs, demands, and criticisms of the NPD parent. However, the fable also offers

57

hope with the Fox, who represents wisdom, as he demonstrates the importance of sharpening one's perception in order to act with a sense of self-preservation. Recognizing the one-way nature of the relationship, he maintains a safe boundary of distance as he enquires after Lion's health.

As the grown child of an NPD parent, you are perhaps well aware of the repeating pattern of interaction that leaves you feeling frustrated, humiliated, manipulated, or simply unrecognized. After your encounters with your NPD parent, you may also feel angry with yourself that you weren't clever enough to avoid taking it on the chin one more time. Growing up in the sphere of an NPD parent has created your inability to recognize that once you enter the domain of the narcissist, the one-way street has no exit.

To recognize the NPD parent's wounding and understand that it exists alongside manipulative behaviors is a difficult picture to accept, since it confronts us with the truth about the NPD parent's limitations to love. Most of us who have had a relationship with an NPD parent will go to the ends of the earth to change this reality about our parent(s).

If you have examined this relationship in therapy, you have most likely heard your therapist gently and repeatedly say, "You know his behaviors really have nothing to do with you. His treatment of you is much more about his need to see himself as competent, successful, or powerful." And, after considering this thought many times, you eventually say to yourself, "Maybe it's really not because of me!" Your emerging recognition of your parent's narcissism is evidence of your growing capacity to validate your own true self. In fact, you are realizing that your NPD parent's criticisms and rejections have had nothing to do with the real you. As your awareness grows, the liberation and relief you feel is your first genuine reward for the healing work you have done.

While writing this book, a client we will call Eileen came in for therapy. In her fifties, Eileen was sensitive and insightful and had done considerable healing work over the course of her life in a twelve-step program and in therapy. She was still distressed, however, that during her visits with her mother, she would feel the resurrection of her intense feelings of inadequacy, anger, and deep longing for love and approval.

She believed that the re-emergence of these powerful feelings was proof to her that she was indeed inadequate since, after all her efforts in therapy, she still felt so many painful feelings.

As our work progressed, I said to her one day, "Eileen, it seems as if you need to believe that you are okay just as you are." Eileen became tearful and said, "You know that is what I remember telling the first therapist I ever saw. I want to feel good about me just for who I am." As she connected this need to the deep loss she had suffered with her mother, she began to understand the significance of growing up with a narcissistic parent. This understanding was a vital healing experience for her because she had never validated or mourned the experiences of wounding that she had gone through with her mother.

At the heart of all the difficulties in growing up with the NPD parent is the common denominator of loss—loss of the unconditional love and recognition for being special, individual, and unique. Without this full validation, she had not been able to let go of the feeling that it was something *in her* that caused her mother to criticize and withhold acceptance and love. In addition, she told herself that she should be able to let go of the strong hurt and anger she felt towards her mother.

Eileen's distress with her mother illustrates the fact that we cannot expect ourselves to move beyond an experience of wounding or hurt until we have fully validated and empathized with the true nature of our wounding. Regardless of progress in other areas of her life, Eileen had not yet understood the depth of her loss. Her issues of wounding had not been completely recognized and mourned, a process that is vital to genuine healing.

With greater recognition and understanding of her mother's narcissism, Eileen began to act on her own behalf, setting limits, asserting her needs, and simply standing her ground. Eileen's ability to take quantum leaps forward in a short period of time was due, for the most part, to all the hard work she had already done. However, this fuller understanding and validation was an imperative part of her final work. She needed to grieve and come to terms with her mother's significant limitations to love her, as well as to recognize and develop abilities for self-care in her relationship with her mother.

Before this final phase of work, Eileen had believed that somehow, if she were truly successful in her healing and growth, she should be unaffected by her mother's hurtful behaviors. The truth is more clearly illustrated by Aesop's fable—a wounded lion is still a lion! While she may have felt sympathy and compassion for her mother, she also needed to respect the power and ability (unconscious though it may be in her mother) to wound her.

If you have grown up with an NPD parent, you have perhaps identified some of your parent's manipulative behaviors that intimidate you into conforming to her wishes or to stay loyal to the family norms. Additionally, you may have recognized how confused you become as you try to sort through the contradictory double messages which leave you feeling uncertain, insecure, and frustrated. Maybe you have had a period of rebellion in your adolescence or even adult life that taught you something about the formidable disapproval you can expect when you assert a disagreement with the NPD parent. Often these periods of rebellion pass and leave an uneasy truce.

Moreover, you may not have realized what your anger was all about. You may have adopted your parent's view point that you were going through an obnoxious phase and believe that you were primarily responsible for the problem. Regardless of your willingness to accept the burden of responsibility, you continue to struggle with your frustration that your NPD parent is unable to acknowledge you and your feelings. Your unacknowledged hurt and anger may leave you stuck in a continuing struggle to gain his or her approval while unable to assert limits and boundaries with this parent.

Frequently, you will vacillate between feelings of anger and frustration on the one hand and the need to idealize your NPD parent on the other. You may idealize him/her for any number of positive traits such as: his impressive accomplishments; her fierce devotion evidenced by her willingness "to do" for you, her fun nature, or her classy style. The list goes on.

As you focus on these larger-than-life qualities in your parent, you also tend to deny or minimize the hurts, disappointments, and manipulations. Perhaps you have an inclination to "forgive and forget" because you realize that your NPD parent had a painful childhood.

Whether the tendency is to idealize the good traits and downplay the negative traits of your NPD parent, or to expect that you should be the bigger person and forgive the hurts, you are probably at war with yourself about how to handle the ongoing relationship. You still haven't figured out a way to peacefully negotiate a satisfying interaction. At the same time, you are having an increasingly difficult time tolerating the one-way street.

In some cases, although you do not deny the hurts, you may repress the intense emotions that are connected to them. Your unacknowledged feelings make you vulnerable to repeating the same family interactions and unable to effectively assert a mature independence and to achieve the healing of self-esteem. In turn, you may have difficulty pursuing goals that are important, including the ability to have a successful relationship of your own. Regardless of the degree of wounding you may have experienced with your NPD parent, you invariably suffer from a range of difficulties relating to low self-esteem, low vitality and initiative, anxiety, or depression.

One way to begin the healing process is to unravel the mystery surrounding the type of projections that were imposed on you from your NPD parent. You may remember from chapter three that a projection is a defense that involves an inability to recognize an aspect of one's self and instead to see or "project" this trait onto someone else. Like the projector in a movie theater we literally see someone else as having a characteristic or set of characteristics that we cannot recognize in ourselves. The less we are able to reflect on our strengths and weaknesses, the less we are able to recognize when we project these qualities onto others. With this capacity failing, we cannot be objective in our assessment of our own and another person's relative strengths and weaknesses. For the narcissist, he has very little (at times, no) self-reflective ability and utilizes the defense of projection to an extreme.

If we recall that the NPD person views another person unconsciously as if this person were an extension of herself, this perception is more powerfully true for his or her children than anyone else. The child, with his vulnerability, openness, and utter dependence, is seen as a "blank check" for the NPD parent to fill in. Depending on a number of factors, such as birth order, gender, and many other circumstances, the

NPD parent will have a varying predisposition to see positive or negative aspects of herself in her child. In fact, if the NPD parent strongly identifies with a given child (whether positively or negatively), that child will receive an intense and confusing array of unconscious projections from the NPD parent.

We must also remember that the child, needing and desiring love, is completely willing to trust the parent and endlessly willing to overlook his parent's shortcomings. In order for the child to cope with the limitations of the NPD parent, he must repress his feelings, wishes, and needs, while adopting the elusive standards of perfection and expectations of his parent. We can see how the powerful defenses and demands of the NPD parent command a high price. At times, this identification on the part of the NPD parent can fully transmit the narcissistic wounding, causing this child to become NPD him or herself.

The intensity of wounding can also be lessened by a number of factors—most importantly, by the positive parenting of another caregiver with a healthier sense of self. Another alleviating element may be due to the "dividing up," so to speak, of the NPD parent's projections among several siblings. Other influences may be the degree to which the NPD parent wishes to be involved with his children or the meaningful involvement of extended family members, friends, or even a teacher who might befriend the child.

Regardless of the degree of wounding, the child, and later the grown child, will invariably suffer a selection of difficulties relating to low self-esteem, low vitality and initiative, anxiety, depression, or difficulties achieving a mutually satisfying relationship with someone. At the end of the day, the dividing line between having the full narcissistic disorder or selected narcissistic traits will rest on your ability to take responsibility for your wounding and initiate those efforts required for healing and growth. This journey towards wholeness has distinct stages and tasks that will be described in depth in chapter five.

Because there are endless scenarios a child might experience with a narcissistic parent or parents, I will only attempt to portray two types of NPD parent/child dynamics: the child who receives the positive projections and the child who receives the negative projections. These two extremes are most aptly illustrated in the children's fairy tales of *Rapunzel* and *Cinderella*. You may identify with a selection of dynamics in each scenario, a blend if you will, due to the endlessly varied expression of the human experience. First, let's glimpse the wisdom of the age-old story that reveals the challenges that occur when the child is given the positive projections of the narcissistic parent.

Rapunzel and the Chosen Child

Rapunzel is the story of a witch who tricks an unsuspecting couple to give up their firstborn child whom she then names Rapunzel. Possessive and insatiable in her need to control her daughter, this NPD mother imprisons Rapunzel in a tall tower that has no exit to the world, only a lofty view from on high. Showered and lavished with apparent love and comforts, Rapunzel is devotedly protected, shielded, and buffered from the harsh realities of the outside world. The witch mother endlessly worships Rapunzel, taking pleasure in her beauty with the daily ritual of combing her long golden hair—an apt metaphor for the child who is given the positive projections. In this scenario, the child is seen as a *positive* extension of the NPD parent—a perfect mirror of her grandiose self.

We can also see the price that is paid. Rapunzel must live in an isolated tower, cut off from the world, with no life of her own or opportunity to experience her own thoughts and feelings. In short, Rapunzel cannot discover and know her true self. Her suffering is a deep longing for something that she can't identify, and she lives her life as if she were asleep, dreaming of realities never lived.

Eventually, a handsome prince discovers Rapunzel singing at her lonely window and falls in love with her. Together they plot to deceive the witch mother and run away. But the witch outwits them and in her rage pushes the prince from the tower where he falls on a bed of thorns and is blinded. She then takes Rapunzel to a remote part of the forest and abandons her. Rapunzel, without warning or preparation, is left to survive in the wilderness alone. As in so many fairy tales, we are not given much clue about her healing journey, but we learn that she gives birth to twins, and in time the lost lovers find each other again. When Rapunzel's tears fall upon her prince's eyes, his sight is restored, and the two live happily together with their reunited family.

Many "chosen" children of NPD parents experience some variation of this controlled, constricted life and encounter an awareness of the true nature of their loss as they taste a more potent experience of life (as we see when Rapunzel meets her prince.) Some crisis occurs that challenges the adult child's long-standing and rigid assumptions of reality. It may be the failure of a love relationship, or the loss of relationship with the NPD parent due to a "falling out," or because of a death. More painful yet may be the loss of the healthier parent. Sometimes the crisis results from disillusionment with the NPD parent and the crumbling of the many idealizations alongside the loss of perceived love. The following story of a client illustrates this unexpected and painful experience.

David, a self-contained and well-regarded physician, came in for therapy one day, as shocked and surprised to find himself in my office as he was by the circumstances that brought him in. He had never given any thought to the idea of therapy, other than to dismiss it as irrelevant, until his life was suddenly turned upside down. He had encountered the full and powerful recognition that his mother's love and all she had done for him had not really been done for him, but instead, for her own needs and desires.

This surprising revelation left him feeling as if the mother (he knew) had died and he had lost connection to the most important person in his life. Alongside his grief and anger, he had intense feelings of self-doubt in his own perceptions of reality, since he had so thoroughly misunderstood his mother. He had lost not only the connection and love he thought he had with his mother, but also a significant part of himself—his trust in his own perceptions.

David had been fighting valiantly to cope with this loss and disorientation on his own until he could no longer deny that his feelings of depression were undermining his ability to function. As he allowed himself the support and help of therapy, he began to sort through the context of his life, validating his abilities and experiences, unhampered by former constraints to censor his perceptions. He began to recognize the depth of his feelings and explore an awareness of himself and his life in ways he had never considered. Before this turning point, he had journeyed through life under the prescriptions of his parents and, most significantly, his NPD mother.

In David's case, he had the common dynamic of having an NPD mother and a passive and withdrawn father who remained subservient to his mother and inaccessible to him. Having such an absent father had required David to turn to his mother for most of his parenting needs, and she in turn focused all her conscious and unconscious expectations on him while devoting herself to *her* goals for him. He needed to grieve the inherent loss of connection with both his parents as well as to recognize and validate his right to discover his true self.

Aside from a period of normal rebellion in adolescence, David had, for the most part, conformed happily to his mother's expectations. He felt fortunate to have the opportunity to pursue a professional career in medicine like his father and to be blessed with such devoted parents. Looking back, David realized that he had been sleepwalking through his life, including one marriage and several long-term relationships. His love for these women had seemingly dissolved over time as he discovered that he had no genuine emotional connection to them. Reflecting on these relationships, he felt he had only been going through the motions without an awareness of his deeper feelings.

David's crisis began when he allowed himself to re-evaluate his career path and leave the medical partnership with his father in their private practice. Only when his mother revealed her intentions to cut him out of her life and prevent him from maintaining other family relationships, did he link former clues he had seen into a deeper understanding of his mother's narcissism.

Without realizing it, David was confronting his entire history of loss and frustration over not having acceptance and support for his own feelings, opinions, and decisions unless they matched those of his mother. Grieving the losses due to his mother's limitation to love also meant grieving his lost opportunities to know himself. David was now able to wrestle consciously with his difficulty feeling confident in his own perceptions of reality, another major theme of struggle for all individuals who have grown up with an NPD parent.

As a child, David needed to give up many of his own feelings and perceptions of reality for the sake of maintaining harmony and receiving acceptance and love from his mother. He had to comply with her expectations or risk losing her love while inviting the criticisms and anger. The lost recognition of his feelings was due to a defense called repression, causing many feelings to remain unconscious or to be forgotten. While he lived in harmony with his mother's wishes, little interfered to call attention to the profound sacrifice he had made.

David's sudden and painful insight had stirred a growing recognition of the many experiences he had never allowed himself to see or feel. He now needed to grieve these losses, acknowledge his anger, and discover his own true feelings about himself and his life. Often in the form of free-floating anxiety, he had to slowly untangle the complex set of unacknowledged feelings he had about himself and his history. He grieved the loss of his former "protected" life and the idealized connections with his parents.

He also learned the difference between loneliness and aloneness. The loneliness—overwhelming at first—was deeply connected and tied to his childhood fears of rejection and abandonment when he did not comply with the expectations of his mother. He began to recognize that these fears were part of a defense that prevented the awareness of his own authentic feelings. As David journeyed into this uncharted territory, validating and empathizing with his true feelings, he retrieved his capacity for empathy, curiosity, passion, and joy.

The tale of *Rapunzel* and David's story reveal what happens to the "chosen" child. Like Rapunzel, some chosen children are never encouraged to aspire to any achievement that will emancipate the child. The NPD parent unconsciously expects this child, once grown, to either remain at home or never stray very far, so that the NPD parent has companionship and can remain in the role of indispensable provider. Even if this adult child does move out of the home, a pattern of ongoing reliance on the NPD parent for financial or emotional support often continues, preventing the adult child from asserting true independence or having a healthy relationship of his or her own.

Although given many of the positive projections of the NPD parent and the benefits that go with it, this child is required to give up his "authentic self" and repress his true feelings so that he can serve his NPD parent's needs. Similar to the narcissist, he maintains an unconscious belief that his authentic self is inherently flawed and shameful. This adult child often walks through life projecting self-confidence but feeling as if he were a fraud. Never having the opportunities to face his own challenges and define his own abilities, he has a deep sense of inadequacy and naturally distrusts those who might expose him. His fear of exposure is at the core of his single-minded purpose to maintain control and be the stage director in most interactions with other people.

This child will inevitably adopt some of the same grandiose feelings and behaviors to compensate for his felt inadequacy. There may also be intermittent or chronic depression. Depression may become the outer symptom that expresses the repressed feelings of hurt, inadequacy, and internalized rage. Perhaps obvious to you by now is how the pattern of narcissistic wounding in the parent is passed on to the child, despite the NPD parent's intention to give opportunities and privileges to his child that he never had himself. In this way, the NPD parent can unwittingly transmit the legacy of narcissistic wounding to his own "chosen" child.

Cinderella and the Rivaled Child

You may immediately recognize that the two main characters in this story reflect the challenge of a child surviving the negative projections of an NPD parent. Destined to an unfortunate fate, Cinderella is named and raised by a cruel stepmother following her real mother's death, her father's unwise selection in remarriage, and his own regrettable premature death. In Cinderella's story, we see the experience of the child who is continually told that she will never amount to anything, while at the same time she is expected *to do* everything. We also see the naked envy of her NPD stepmother as she puts Cinderella down in the eyes of others and attempts to elevate the attributes of her own daughters.

For the NPD mother, Cinderella embodies all the wished-for traits that she has unconsciously repressed and denied in herself: sensitivity, empathy, and a thoughtful and caring nature. Cinderella also receives the projected envy for these qualities and becomes an object to be rivaled against. Under the weight of the negative projections, this child must contend with regular criticisms, humiliations, and punishments— overt, in the form of beatings and unfair treatment—or covert, in the form of denied comforts and safety. The NPD stepmother sees her treatment of Cinderella as perfect justice for the negative characteristics she is so convinced belong to this child. Perhaps the mere status of being a child is reason enough for the NPD parent to heap hardship and abuse (emotional and/or physical) upon the child. The NPD parent often views the helpless vulnerability of the child with unconscious contempt because she has completely repressed and disowned any experience of this painful history in herself.

Left alone and under siege, this child must tap into her inner self for inventive means of survival and often becomes resourceful and determined—illustrated perhaps by the metaphor of turning pumpkins into carriages and mice into footmen. Yet the untold side of this fairytale is the anger and rage Cinderella must feel for the endless insults to her dignity and integrity as a human being. How could Cinderella be anything but enraged by receiving such prolonged abuse and unfair treatment? For the "rivaled-against" child, this unresolved anger will lead to some form of chronic or acute depression in adult life and a repeating struggle for positive mutual regard in her relationships. At the end of the story, we are given a hint of the anger Cinderella must feel with the sweet revenge of her stepmother's humiliation as she awkwardly attempts to have the glass slipper placed on her daughters' overlarge feet. The untold story in *Cinderella* is the fact that her anger must be dealt with if she is to live happily into the future.

One client who experienced this painful existence is a young woman I will call Amy, the only child of a nurturing, but passive mother, and the unfortunate inheritor of her NPD father's negative projections. A successful and worldly power broker in business and politics, her father had survived against impressive odds as a child himself. He had not only survived profound poverty, but also a history of intense emotional and physical wounding at the hands of his own father. However, because he had repressed and denied this emotional pain, he had *idealized this hardship as the conditions that created his strengths,* honed his abilities to achieve, and ultimately provided his purpose in life—to champion the underdog.

His drive to succeed, in turn, protected and helped him to maintain his denial of all the painful feelings he had never allowed himself to acknowledge or work through. In this context, we can begin to make sense of how he viewed his parenting role with Amy. Perceiving his own history as positive, he consciously justified his desire to recreate the same circumstances for his daughter's development and to motivate her to serve the same "just causes."

Although a successful businessman, he was determined to raise his family in a dangerous inner-city neighborhood, making his children an even greater target for aggression due to their obvious difference in economic stature. He was completely unconscious that these beliefs were defensive rationalizations, thinly veiled excuses to act out his own aggression and anger for all the abuse he had suffered. He was similarly unaware that his desire to motivate his daughter to "join the cause" was due to his need to create a perfect mirror of his grandiose self.

Throughout Amy's life, she heard how her father's triumph over adversity had shaped him into becoming a superior person. Only when she met the same "test of metal" by overcoming the difficult circumstances he purposely set up for her, would she be worthy of his respect, approval, and acceptance. The confusing experience of his relentless criticisms and purposeful barriers, alongside the promise of being one of the "chosen" people who triumph over hardship, seemed an ingenious design to destroy the sanity of any human being, let alone a child. How indeed can a child be anything but confused and angered by the fact that her father, who claims to love her, would purposefully subject her to extreme adversity and painful experiences, all in the name of her own welfare? If it weren't for the sake of her ability to take refuge in her mother's nurturing comfort, she would probably not have survived physically or psychologically.

Amy's mother, the passive, depressive, other-parent figure in the dyad of the NPD parent relationship, had long since conceded her reality to her NPD spouse. Depending on the severity of this passivity, this parent will, to varying degrees, temper the impact of the NPD parent. In Amy's case, her mother assumed the exclusive role of homemaker and caregiver. While offering Amy an important refuge of comfort, she was unable to offer an alternative model of a capable and competent person.

Whenever Amy attempted to secure or maintain her own goals, her father would "raise the bar," so to speak, like the stepmother in *Cinderella* pretending to let her go to the ball if she finished a greater number of chores. When Amy succeeded in getting all A's in her classes, her father broke the promise he had made to enroll her in a more challenging and safe school that she had wished to attend. Little surprise that this endless no-win situation caused Amy to angrily act out all of her father's negative projections. Like many children caught in such a double bind, they often turn to the revenging behaviors of becoming the "bad child"—outdoing, if they can, the NPD parent's worst projections. In adolescence, Amy began to skip school, take drugs, and turn to other rebellious teenagers for companionship and belonging.

By the time Amy passed through adolescence, she was struggling with many inner conflicts, among them her disillusionment about her ability to accomplish her own dreams. Depleted by the ravages of unmet needs, negative projections, and finally her own self-destructive behaviors, she was now seeking solace through relationships with men who were as severe and harsh in their narcissistic tendencies as her father. In this way she was re-enacting the negative experience of her childhood—her dependence on a tyrannical narcissistic father.

This adult child will often experience some form of burnout in early adult life that will allow her to recognize her need for healing. The final crisis for Amy was the devastating impact of losing a relationship with an idealized lover. Once Amy could no longer deny the pattern and consequences of her childhood wounding, she allowed herself to seek therapy. At this point, she was severely depressed and questioning her very sanity. We may not be surprised that Amy had arrived at such a state of fragmentation, since she had literally been through a lifetime of struggle, alongside the inevitable loss of any outside validation.

Sometimes the child who receives the negative projections may adopt the same defenses as the NPD parent by repressing the feelings of hurt and rage. In addition, the child may idealize the NPD parent and believe in the parent's portrayal of his grandiose self. In this way, the grown child desperately clings to the wished-for love from the NPD parent, wards off the painful feelings of earlier trauma, and inherits the narcissistic defense, for the most part, full scale.

On the other hand, the adult child may *not* harbor any illusions that the NPD parent behaved as he did for her own good and will channel the grit and determination that it took to survive such wounding into a competitive drive to succeed and outdo the NPD parent on the parent's own turf. Many "rivaled-against" adult children strive to excel in their family business or another enterprise, hoping to surpass the NPD parent's success in order to gain approval, revenge, or both!

As Amy put it, "I always know that when I am with my father, one of us will end up playing the role of king of the universe while the other will have to be a lowly worm. At least I get my turn to play king of the universe these days." Then with obvious sadness she continues, "There is never any in-between with us. We can never relate as equals." Despite all the anger and rage, she still had a deep longing for acceptance and love.

As Amy dealt with her feelings of anger, sadness, and her own sense of inadequacy, she was able to identify patterns of narcissistic wounding that led to her self-sabotaging behaviors. Fortunately for Amy, her natural gifts and abilities for self-reflection allowed her to change and heal the pattern of wounding which was delivered to her so intensely. Like the "chosen" child, she had the difficult task of differentiating her natural desires and honest feelings from those connected to her anger and drive to compete with her father.

Although the experience of the "rivaled-against" child stands in vivid contrast to that of the "chosen" child, she too will strive for the elusive substitutes for self in order to gain the unmet needs for acknowledgment and respect. Additionally, she will wish to avenge herself in order to express the anger and hurt for such mistreatment and wounding.

*In both types of experience, the "rivaled-against child" and the "chosen child" are forced to cope with the powerful projections of the NPD parent by responding **compliantly** or **defiantly** and pay the inevitable price involved— giving up the true self.*

As mentioned previously, these two depictions of wounding are only a few of the scenarios that the NPD parent will potentially play out with her child or children. In circumstances of more than one child, the projections of the NPD parent will often be diluted because they are divided up. In addition, sometimes one child receives a greater degree of the unconscious projections from the NPD parent while the remaining siblings are, in a sense, spared. The degree to which a child receives the NPD parent's projections will be related to how strongly the NPD parent identifies with the child, regardless of whether this identification is positive or negative.

Other siblings who watch from the sidelines may feel enormous envy and contempt for the child who is given the positive projections of the NPD parent, mistakenly believing that this child is gaining an unfair advantage. This perspective is certainly understandable since the other siblings are frequently ignored or dismissed altogether. Consequently, attention, money, privileges, etc., become the all-important currency of love in the relationship with the NPD parent. Siblings, like starving children, end up fighting for the scraps from the table of the NPD parent. Ironically, the less acknowledged children are sometimes spared the more intense wounding from the NPD parent despite this apparent loss of attention. Left on their own, these siblings have more freedom to discover their true selves because they are unimpeded by the NPD parent to follow their own impulses, intuitions, and inspirations.

Another variation of the *Cinderella* theme is the example of the codependent child who is expected to be endlessly aware of the needs of the parent and at the same time remains deprived of any recognition for her own needs. This child gains status and self-esteem from the NPD parent based on her ability "to do for" this parent and will develop the characteristics commonly known as codependency. In effect, this child instinctively recognizes that only after her NPD mother has had her meal will she have hope of finding some food for herself. She continually walks the tightrope of delaying her own gratification in the hope that something will be there for her later. Eventually she will lose sight of her own feelings and needs while developing an extraordinary ability for intuiting the feelings and needs of others. Indeed, we can see the inevitable origin of codependency, as this child moves away from her true self with a substitute self that focuses on others—the false self that is "other" focused.

The trap of this adult child's wounding can also be formidable, as he or she is unable to recognize that the empathy so intensely felt for others is an extension of the lost empathy for the self. This adult child will often give her "self" over to the grandiose self of the narcissistic individual. Caught in the vicious cycle of seeking a substitute self-esteem that is dependent on the need to care for another person, this adult child can also remain blind to the healing so necessary for whole-ness.

Meanwhile the "chosen" child has paid the price for his special sta-tus and may discover only by accident that he has been wounded at all. Appearing to be the proverbial "spoiled" child, others interpret his moody irritability as an impossible-to-please temperament, unaware of the many times that the NPD parent has interfered with his attempts to be his own person. If you were there to observe, you might feel compelled to say, "Let the poor child do it for himself!" The labeling of spoiled is, indeed, unfair, since this child too is not given what he needs. Instead, he is given an abundance of what he doesn't need.

Imagine for a moment being given a gift that is completely un-wanted on your part and perhaps at some expense and effort on the part of the giver. Your conflicted feelings of disappointment, frustra-tion, guilt, and the oppressive burden of pretending, as well as the disgust or resentment that this person is so out of tune with you, are a few of the internalized emotions that the "spoiled" child feels. In addition, this child internalizes deep feelings of inadequacy because he has not been able to discover his own choices and abilities for himself—especially in his interactions with others. Fearful of interacting with the world, he appears shy, moody, and at times irregular in his behaviors with his friends.

When an over-gratifying NPD parent intrudes upon his child, this child naturally moves further inward, shunning the experience of con-tact and connection with others. Later in life, the grown child fears being overpowered by others, especially in his intimate relationships. Denied the ability to struggle for his own sense of competence in relat-ing to others, this child will internalize his own standards (generally grandiose) and compete with himself to beat his own best score. He seeks interaction and feedback from others primarily to validate this accomplishment and rarely feels satisfied with the reward, no matter how good it is. He has internalized his NPD parent's grandiose self and lost the ability to enjoy the fulfillment of his own feelings. The compul-sion to achieve the illusory perfect standards of his NPD parent's false self has now become his own. His lack of empathy for others is the consequence of his inability to know empathy for himself, or even the fact that he was denied empathy and recognition for his true self.

In each scenario, we can see the tradeoffs and ultimately the terrible prices that are paid with wounding to the self. Whatever unique wounding exists for you as the adult child of an NPD parent, there will be some manifestation of difficulty in the form of compulsive behaviors, grandiose strivings, low self-esteem, excessive guilt and worry, anxiety, depression, loss of vitality, codependency issues—and the list goes on. These symptoms will be the clues that force your attention inward to recognize your need for healing.

Alongside the symptoms are messages that contain a deeper truth about the self, a truth that forces the awareness of wounding and the need for healing. The most imperative first step is to acknowledge the symptom and allow the discovery process to unfold—a mysterious and unacknowledged story waiting to be understood. Whatever circumstances prompt this recognition, the window of opportunity for healing does exist. To experience the joy and fulfillment of greater wholeness, you must courageously step into this unknown territory and claim your *true self* and your *life*.

CHAPTER FOUR SUMMARY

Aesop's fable of The Old Lion and the Fox is a powerful metaphor for the child's relationship with the NPD parent because it demonstrates the painful themes of interaction in this relationship. First we see the theme of wounding as the child is compelled to sacrifice his or her "true self" for the endless needs and expectations of the NPD parent. Then we see the boundaries that are so necessary for protection when dealing with the NPD parent to prevent the continuation of this wounding process.

As the adult child begins to recognize the truth of her own wounding with the NPD parent, she can begin to heal and grow. Healing and growth will be reflected when:

- The adult child can validate and empathize with the thoughts and feelings that are expressions of her authentic self and mourn the loss of these opportunities in childhood.

- The adult child can develop protective boundaries—asserting limits on the entitlement demands and devaluing behaviors of the NPD parent.

The beginning of all healing must start with awareness and the retrieval of our authentic thoughts and feelings. The many lost opportunities to explore and know the self are important to grieve. In other words, the adult child must validate and empathize with his or her genuine feelings and with the lost opportunity to feel unconditional love.

Other important clues for the adult child to identify are the type of "projections" he or she has experienced from the NPD parent (or continues to experience if the NPD parent is still living). Because the narcissist sees others as extensions of his own self, every adult child has received a certain selection of projections from the narcissistic parent(s). Projections are characteristics that the NPD parent has repressed or disowned in himself and instead sees in (projects onto) the child. Because these projections have little to do with the true self of the child, the child is forced to respond to these projections compliantly (striving to manifest them) or defiantly (striving to fight against them).

We discussed two fairytales that are apt illustrations of the contrasting experiences of being given the positive and negative projections in *Rapunzel* and *Cinderella*.

- The "chosen" child (given the positive projections) is over-protected and over-gratified while molded to reflect the NPD parent's grandiose self.

- The "rivaled-against" child (given the negative projections) is expected to be a failure and meanwhile expected "to do" everything or serve the NPD parent.

Although these are merely examples of two extremes, these stories reveal the intense wounding that occurs when an NPD parent identifies with his/her child either positively or negatively. Those siblings that are dismissed and ignored often feel great resentment and jealousy of the "chosen" sibling(s), rarely realizing that they are in a sense being spared a more difficult wounding. These children have the advantage of knowing that they are being wounded and the freedom to explore their own impulses and feelings. Regardless of the different experiences for siblings with an NPD parent, it is not uncommon for one of the NPD parent's children to develop the full manifestation of the narcissistic personality disorder.

If the adult child has survived with a healthier sense of self than the NPD parent, there are inevitably a number of painful problems that he or she may suffer from, such as anxiety, depression, low self-esteem, reduced energy and vitality for life, compulsive behaviors, addictions, chronic illnesses, and relationship difficulties. The specific "symptom" can offer the gift of awareness and ultimately the choice to begin healing. Without the commitment to heal, we are destined to repeat some painful version of the struggle that we encountered in childhood. The journey to wholeness for the adult child is discussed in depth in chapter five.

You're Not in Kansas Anymore

The Healing Journey for the "Adult Child" of the NPD Parent

The turning point towards healing is a mysterious and often exciting passage. Like the feelings before a rainstorm, a heaviness hangs in the air, then a sudden drop in pressure and a gathering of forces transforms the clouds into a chorus of raindrops. Our psyche resembles this process as it signals a readiness to cleanse itself. Sometimes a crisis is the catalyst for this healing opportunity, yet other times only one small painful event occurs in a long cascade of similar events. Somehow this particular moment triggers a feeling of imperative need—the drive to break through the defenses and begin the journey of healing.

The Defenses

Our psychological defenses can be compared to our skin; we are not conscious of their presence. Once needed in childhood to survive, we continue to employ these defenses in adult life with almost no awareness that we are doing so. Sigmund Freud once likened these defenses to the 15th century man's suit of armor. While a man living in the 15th century might require the use of such a defense to survive, we can see that this same individual taken forward in time to the 21st century will experience his armor as an outdated clumsy barrier. Similar to the knight's armor, the defenses we develop in childhood become the primary source of self-sabotaging behaviors in adult life, interfering with our ability to achieve the goals we seek.

Few of us in our early adult years are aware that these defenses exist, let alone the powerful role they play in our lives, directing our behaviors, influencing our interpretations of others and, most importantly, causing us to replay old and painful scenarios. Only by the time we are well into our twenties or thirties do we begin to recognize these powerful unconscious forces. Finally, *even when we do see that our history is negatively impacting our behaviors, choices, and feelings, we must confront the unspoken commandment of our families and our culture to not look, not explore, and not know our deeper self.*

The refrain I hear again and again from individuals is the argument, "Why should I look at my past? I don't want to blame my parents." Or "Why should I dwell on the past? It's over and in the past. What good will it do to go back to all that?" Or "My childhood was great. My parents were wonderful! I'm not going to find fault with them when they gave me everything they could," and so on. Maybe you have experienced some of these conscious rationalizations that discourage you from exploring your history, saying to yourself it is disloyal, nonproductive, weak, ungrateful, etc. Consequently, like the thunderstorm, the feelings that compel us to push through our rationalizations must gather a certain force to break through such pervasive taboos. Otherwise, our faintheartedness will allow us to give up and run at the first revelation of old pain seeking its opportunity for validation and healing.

For these reasons, the assistance and support of a competent therapist is strongly recommended and often required. While we may find empathy and support in a friend or a support group, rarely can we look to these individuals for the gentle but firm push we need to confront the hidden feelings, defenses, and behaviors in ourselves. In addition, we may invariably ally with other individuals who assist us in minimizing the deeper issues, reinforcing the impulse to grasp the "quick fix," glossing over our problems with simplistic psychological recipes. Sometimes the process of working in therapy can itself be a new version of avoiding the healing we need if the therapist has not worked through his or her own personal issues. The critical evaluation process of finding the therapist who can help you with the problems or goals that you identify is addressed in the appendix.

The Truth of Deeper Wounding

Pain is often the unwelcome herald of needed change. Pain also insists that this change be given the attention it deserves, which is generally far more than we want to acknowledge. Symptom relief is, therefore, usually the primary goal most of us desire when we first seek the help of a professional. Yet, to merely seek the short-term goal of eliminating a painful symptom rarely achieves the healing we require. An example of the distinction I am making is illustrated through the experience of a client I will call Jane.

An attractive attorney in her forties, Jane came into therapy because of her feelings of hopelessness about her marriage of nine years. She had tried many times to gain her husband's cooperation in attending marital therapy, as well as a number of other attempts to address the many problems in their relationship. He had, however, remained unwilling to join her in these efforts.

At this point, the recognition of her desire for a divorce caused intense feelings of depression and guilt. This would be Jane's second divorce, and she was feeling a significant sense of failure and shame about a second marriage failing. The symptoms identified by Jane were primarily her guilt, self-doubt, and subsequent depression over her inability to carry out a decision that she knew in her heart was right. Although she knew what she wanted to do about her marriage, the feelings of guilt and shame were almost intolerable. By assisting Jane so that she could proceed with this needed change, I would probably have helped her alleviate her guilt, shame, and loss over a second divorce. However, by ignoring the opportunity to understand the recurring dynamic in her relationships, Jane would be susceptible to repeating this scenario again in a future relationship.

As Jane allowed herself to explore a deeper understanding of her symptoms, she began to recognize that her husbands were uncanny reflections of her difficult and painful relationship with her narcissistic, volatile father. From an early age, she had been the recipient of his harsh demands, criticisms, and dark moods due to his many narcissistic traits and the additional deteriorating influence of his alcoholism.

Jane had struggled with issues of low self-esteem and a desperate desire to feel loved. Her tendency to choose men with deep emotional disturbances who in turn reinforced her belief that she was responsible for their well-being was a pattern that she began to identify in therapy. Jane was able to see that her feelings of guilt were also reflective of a more intense wounding—her own painful history in childhood, which she had never had the opportunity to fully explore, understand, and mourn.

Because I am so often dismayed by the endlessly creative efforts that friends, family members, and clients use to circumvent this imperative healing process, I am compelled to state that this resistance is our own worst enemy. In fact, our resistance to journey more deeply into ourselves lies at the very heart of our arrested growth. This resistance to explore our inner emotions is primarily due to our fear and reluctance to face feelings that at one time in our life were so overwhelming and painful that we developed defenses to protect us from even knowing they exist.

Furthermore, you may be surprised to learn that an early trauma or unmet need in childhood is not, in truth, the most significant wound. For instance, the death of a parent, the unpredictable rages, or even the neglect of a parent is not necessarily the most damaging contribution in the experience of wounding. *While these events may be the source of the wound, the greater wound is the lack of opportunity or support for the child to deal with her feelings about these events. This lack of opportunity to experience her natural emotional response transforms the trauma or hurt into one of greater permanence.* In other words, the necessity for the child to employ a defense, which disconnects her from knowing her feelings, or perhaps even remembering these experiences, is the unhealed scar that will surface later in life in the form of some painful re-enactment or symptom.

Imagine a child who has lost a parent through death or abandonment. This child will have significant feelings of sadness, anger, hurt, and rejection but will have little insight or awareness that these feelings are flooding in on her. If this child were to have a supportive, sympathetic parent figure who could help validate her feelings and encourage her to talk about them, she would be able to retain a healthy sense of confidence in her ability to respond to her life with all the natural responses and feelings that her psyche is experiencing. She would be able to know, express, and normalize her feelings, internalizing an ability to have empathy for herself. She would no doubt have the painful challenge of coming to terms with a difficult loss and additional challenges in childhood; however, with the opportunity to know and express her feelings, she is allowed to proceed through her childhood with her sense of "self" intact.

On the other hand, the child who is thwarted from identifying and experiencing her feelings (either because the adults around her don't recognize this need or because their own needs demand the child attend to them instead) will be forced to employ powerful defenses to prevent her awareness of these feelings. The child's internalized command to shut down her awareness of her own feelings is, in a sense, the necessary unnatural response to the circumstances she is living with. A parent's inability to empathize with or recognize a child's feelings and individuality is an unnatural form of parenting; the child's only recourse is to protect herself from repeated injury by using an unnatural tool—a defense mechanism.

In a sense, our psyche can be compared to clay. A wound or painful event(s) in childhood is like an imprint, the impact of which alters the child in the same way that an imprint on clay changes its shape. However, our feeling response to this event, like the malleability of clay, will have a great deal to do with the lasting impression of such a wound. The ongoing support and acknowledgment of the child's feelings is analogous to moistening the clay, thereby increasing the possibility of reshaping it after the impact of a significant hurt. On the other hand, preventing or not assisting the child in acknowledging and expressing her feelings surrounding this painful experience will result in a defense mechanism similar to the hardening of the clay after an imprint has occurred. Once the clay has hardened, the process of reshaping it will be much more difficult.

Now, it may be obvious that a parent who repeatedly rages against or neglects his child will most likely be a parent who is unable and unwilling to help the child with her feelings about these behaviors. Indeed, this is probably true. However, the presence of a "safe" adult or parent figure in the child's life (a person who can supportively listen to the child) can play a vital role in reducing the impact of these painful events. This crucial element may explain some of the mystery as to why one child in a family survives with a sense of self and vitality, and another child does not fare as well. Perhaps the presence of a doting grandparent or a neighbor helped one sibling while another sibling did not have this support. Or perhaps one sibling came along at a later age for the parent, a time when this parent was more open and supportive of hearing her child's expression of feelings (or the reverse if the parent is experiencing a progressive disease of addiction).

Whatever the circumstances are for the growing child, unique differences will play a significant role regarding issues of wounding and the development of defenses. The importance in all of this is to recognize that *issues of wounding are critically tied to our lost opportunities for dealing with our feelings and, therefore, to our inability to have empathy for others and ourselves. The defenses, which once protected us, are now the barriers preventing us from finding deeper fulfillment and intimacy in our lives.*

The Symptom

The formation of the powerful defenses necessary to protect the child from his feelings will require enormous psychological energy, reducing his choices and flexibility for future experiences in life. In addition, the child's unconscious mind will form a distorted meaning from the childhood losses or traumas, causing him to internalize negative false beliefs about himself. For instance, the child who has lost a parent may internalize an unconscious belief that he is unlovable or that he is flawed in some way and that this perceived flaw is the cause of such an unhappy event. This false self-perception along with the fear of his own feelings is the mortar and brick of his defenses.

From this point on, fear takes over and causes him to try and prevent future abandonment. This fear (whether conscious or unconscious) will inevitably manifest a replay of abandonment again and again. Fear in this context is a defense, which holds us hostage, not allowing us to move beyond it because, in reality, it is protecting us from knowing our feelings about the original trauma. As Annie Rogers states in her remarkable book, *A Shining Affliction,* "What we fear most has already happened." Only when we have uncovered the buried feelings connected to the original wounding experiences are we liberated to a future free of painful re-enactments or painful symptoms.

Children are, of course, unprepared to deal with many of the tasks involved with independence and interdependence. As parents and adults, we realize this and assist them everyday in this learning process. Still, in the area of feelings, we often overlook and deny this help. Here, of course, we have the vicious cycle of our own learned denial and difficulty knowing our feelings, which we now transmit to our children. We may employ endless rationalizations and at times remain oblivious to our lack of empathy and support when our child is overcome by frustration, or exasperated and hurt by our unwillingness to hear and understand something he is trying to communicate.

At this point, we are replaying some of the same wounding messages to our children that were once delivered to us. Despite our recognition of the echoes of past behaviors we once abhorred in our parents, we find ourselves unable to change or eliminate these patterns in ourselves. Whenever we lack empathy for our children or someone else (provided we acknowledge it), we can begin to recognize that we are in close proximity to a deeper connection with our own childhood wounding.

The child who has paid the price of shutting down the feelings of hurt and pain is the adult who remains hostage to the blackmail of his defense mechanisms. The ransom is the damage that our defenses do to others or ourselves. For example, we may regularly displace or project our feelings onto others, or instead internalize our feelings causing a depletion of confidence and energy for life. Perhaps our unacknowledged feelings manifest themselves in the form of chronic irritability, depression, or a negative outlook.

Alice Miller succinctly delineates the wounding process in her extraordinary book, *For Your Own Good*, as follows:

"The individual psychological stages in the lives of most people are:

1. To be hurt as a small child without anyone recognizing the situation as such

2. To fail to react to the resulting suffering with anger

3. To show gratitude for what are supposed to be good intentions

4. To forget everything

5. To discharge the stored-up anger onto others in adulthood or to direct it against oneself."

The primary hope we have of changing these wounding patterns rests in our ability to become consciously aware that our defenses are sabotaging our lives. I once heard of a psychoanalyst who was famous for his parting ritual. He would shake a person's hand and say, "May you have a good nightmare!" This odd-sounding goodbye reflected his belief that only when we are pushed to the wall by our pain from within, will we face the unresolved issues that reside under the surface of our defenses. The sufficiently painful "nightmare" that demands our attention to wake up is also our greatest ally, as it signals the beginning of this journey.

In the same way, our psyches will push us from within to face our history and the legacy of our parent's history. The push is usually in the form of a psychological or relationship crisis. The inevitable first step is finding the courage to face our inner self in a much deeper way than we may have been willing to face before. Once we have a crisis that we cannot ignore—whether it is a relationship failure, depression, or unrelenting anxiety—we may finally allow ourselves permission to look further into our psyches and seek help in therapy.

If you grew up with one or more narcissistic parents, you are probably familiar with confusion and questions like, "What do I really want?" or "Who am I?" Alongside this confusion is often the struggle of living out the "shoulds" or expectations of others (especially your parents') in contrast to your own impulse to explore, experiment, and take risks based on your feelings and desires. One day, a female client reflected back on her first awareness that she had given too much of her life over to the wants, needs, and expectations of her NPD mother and said, "When I finally realized that it was going to be either her life or mine—

I decided it was going to be my life!" This was a turning point for this client, who then began the difficult but life-renewing process of self-discovery. Her decision also meant that she begin to set limits on what her mother dictated about her life.

The Healing

Grieving the losses of early childhood is the heart of the healing work we must do. The beginning stages of this process are undeniably the most difficult. When we first begin to feel some of the intense feelings we have repressed from childhood, we feel a natural fear that somehow our pain will be limitless. Countless clients have said to their therapists, "I'm afraid if I let myself cry, I will never stop!" Fear of being overwhelmed is the unavoidable demon we must wrestle with as we open the door to the truth of our unacknowledged feelings.

Of course, the fact that we now admit that we have such powerful and frightening feelings undermines the denial that says we are doing just fine. We are recognizing the presence of something important that needs attention. And yet each step of the journey can be the place where we lack courage, refusing to go on while succumbing to our fears. At any point, we can choose the path of least resistance, give our defenses credibility and ignore the feelings within that are pushing for acknowledgment.

Men, in particular, balk at the notion of recovering their emotional lives. After all, men, who were once little boys, had many more lessons instructing them to ignore their feelings while exalting the importance of not feeling—as if this were a virtue of strength. Despite our current age of enlightenment, this cultural norm is perhaps as strong as ever. Men are therefore intuitively aware of how unprepared they are to traverse this uncharted world. Therapists must offer regular support as the process of healing work unfolds, reassuring the client that emotional healing is a slow, step-by-step process.

A little at a time, we discover a new feeling and begin to connect it to a growing awareness of our history. A little at a time, we discover our ability to identify our feelings and give them a voice. A little at a time, we discover that our feelings of anger, depression, sorrow, or humiliation do not overwhelm us or remain a constant unwelcome visitor. These feelings, like any other feelings, will wax and wane like the coming and going of the tide. Fears of our feelings, however, will cause us to fixate them in our minds, believing them to be terminal conditions or overwhelming monsters.

Each time we express and release some of these painful feelings, we gain confidence in our ability to regroup after a period of emotional work in therapy. We begin to allow ourselves to enter into this process more freely. Whether we are a CEO, teacher, mother, doctor, or student trying to maintain a challenging life full of responsibilities, we gradually discover that we will not have to drop out of our duties or pursuits in life to do this healing work. In fact, we recognize the enormous benefit of embarking on this path because we now glimpse greater feelings of aliveness and spontaneity. We begin to feel the reward of getting in touch with a truer experience of life.

For some individuals, a sudden crisis may precipitate a more dramatic deterioration that requires the temporary intense efforts of therapy, and initially takes time away from daily life. These scenarios rarely occur, however, and generally reflect a longstanding lack of opportunity, or sometimes unwillingness for any inner exploration.

A middle-aged man I will call Joe faced his need for deeper healing after realizing in marital therapy that his history was not the idealized version he had consciously nurtured for so long. As he began to surface his repressed feelings of humiliation, hurt, and loneliness resulting from a protracted childhood illness, alongside the harsh negativity of his NPD father, he began to experience the full range of feelings involved in such losses. The first few days following our sessions, he often felt depressed, which caused him to fear getting trapped in depression and unable to maintain his hard-driving career. Soon, however, he realized that these were normal episodes in the healing process that would not last or threaten his daily functioning. Gradually, he became more comfortable accessing the feelings he had as a child, as well as an adult. Joe's courage to work on his emotional healing transformed his inability to have closeness and intimacy with his wife into a relationship with more fulfilling connection.

A common trap for us on the healing journey is to remain in the intellectual realm, focusing primarily on analytic insight. Many therapists are willing to let the therapeutic work become primarily an intellectual insight-oriented process. In other words, you might gain a wealth of understanding without resolving your deeper feelings. This is so common that I am often prepared to make the case to a client that he or she has barely opened the door to true healing since the journey is ultimately an emotional one—with insight serving merely as the road map. A skilled therapist who knows how to balance artful listening, guidance, gentle pushes to go deeper, and many more opportunities for empathic silence, is a rare combination. This is primarily true because many therapists themselves have not traveled fully into their deeper histories of emotional wounding to reconnect to their repressed feelings. The trap of believing we have completed our emotional healing because we have gained insight and intellectual understanding can be as compelling to the therapist as it can to the client.

Although more rare, the trap at the other end of the continuum of the healing process is getting in touch with feelings for feelings' sake. There are therapies or therapy methods that may contribute to the destructive process of focusing on the expression of feelings as the end goal of the healing work. As a result, an individual can become caught up in an effort for emotional release as the only valid purpose of getting in touch with the true self. On the contrary, this is simply another way that the individual may be indulging in a substitute self, avoiding the more specific nature of wounding through a lack of integration with intellectual insight. The best verifying evidence that we are on the right track in our healing process is an increasing clarity about our feelings, which is the result of both insight and our connection to our emotions.

Several years ago, a young woman came into therapy seeking relief from her panic attacks. Because she was handling her life efficiently and was a strong skeptic of psychology, she immediately resisted any attempt to look deeper into her history. Recognizing her potential short stay in therapy, I decided to cut to the chase and interpret my intuitive hunch. I said to her that she certainly must have had a hard time dealing with anger since she was so overwhelmed by fear. While I may or may not have been correct with this interpretation, the only way she could find out was to discover her own feelings and gain some sense of internal validation.

When we met the following week, she reported with somewhat quizzical surprise and delight with herself that she had a powerful dream in which she intensely vented her rage at her boss (who had been putting her through considerable hell for an entire year). Not long after this validating experience, she also began to connect her repressed feelings of anger and sadness to the lifelong waxing and waning of her anxiety symptoms. Eventually, she was also able to acknowledge and mourn the issues of wounding that she had experienced in her childhood.

Whatever the therapist may interpret or theorize as we proceed on our journey, the healing work is ultimately born out of our own discoveries that clearly and unmistakably connect us to our feelings, much like the tactile sensation of a puzzle piece snapping into place.

The Problem of Premature Forgiveness

Grieving the losses and wounding in childhood may also involve recognizing the unresolved losses our parents suffered in their own childhood. As we see past the brambles of our own defenses, we can also see past the defenses of our parents. Yet again, this is another place we can get stuck if we are not careful.

Although we have gained the credible sense that our symptoms have a deeper connection to how our parent(s) cared for us in childhood, we may now hit the wall of our desire to protect our parents from any self-reproach. We want to protect them from "blame" and again fall back into our defense of denial. We would often prefer to believe that somehow we were the cause of this painful parenting or stick to the clichés that "our parents did the best they could," rather than look directly into our feelings of hurt and anger. In addition, we have multiple messages from society and religious teachings that tell us the only way to release these feelings is through forgiveness. Here, Alice Miller again makes a compelling case in her powerful book, *For Your Own Good*.

"Genuine forgiveness does not deny anger but faces it head-on." She makes the point over and over again that when our history of childhood wounding is uncovered, then the repressed anger or rage will give way to the grief and sorrow that our parents were unable to treat us differently. At this point we can truly gain insight into our parent's childhood and experience genuine, mature sympathy. Alice Miller illustrates throughout all her books that the child's natural response to parental demands is to always try to understand and accept the parent's narcissistic expectations as a matter of course.

> "But he has to pay for this pseudo-understanding with his feelings and his sensitivity to his own needs, i.e., with his authentic self. This is why access to the normal, angry, uncomprehending, and rebellious child he once was had previously been blocked off. When this child within the adult is liberated, he will discover his vital roots and strength.... To be free to express resentment dating back to early childhood does not mean that one now becomes a resentful person, but rather the exact opposite."

For the very reason that we are permitted to experience these feelings that were once felt, but not allowable, we are liberated from the chain of our costly defenses and symptoms. Again, Alice Miller states:

> "For these reasons I believe that the free expression of resentment against one's parents represents a great opportunity. It provides access to one's true self, reactivates numbed feelings, opens that way for mourning and...with luck...reconciliation. In any case, it is an essential part of the process of psychic healing."

Our Parents and the Here and Now

Once we have broken through our denial, and we are willing to acknowledge our feelings towards our parents, we can anchor and enhance our progress by initiating a dialogue with them, even if they are no longer living, and we can only do this at their gravesides. The open articulation of feelings with the NPD parent is an important part of the healing process, and we may choose between essentially two levels to undertake this work. Ideally, you will do both.

The first level is the full articulation of hurt, anger, embarrassment, or fear connected to your parent's narcissistic behaviors throughout your childhood. Creating the opportunity to address issues of this magnitude with your NPD parent involves deep personal choice and requires careful considerations about the unique dynamics of your relationship with your parents. *The second level of work with the NPD parent is targeting specific interaction patterns in your present relationship which continue to be painful or frustrating and developing specific skills to "reshape" your NPD parent's behaviors.* As I have mentioned before in previous examples, either choice you make will require mental and emotional rehearsal in a safe and supportive environment so that you can gain the confidence and readiness you need to achieve these goals.

The mere process of examining your choices about which level you wish to address in the "here and now" with your NPD parent(s) will facilitate a fuller ability on your part to heal. For instance, many of us encounter feelings of guilt as soon as we begin to talk with a therapist about our feelings of anger and hurt with our parent(s). These and many other confused and difficult feelings will surface as you consider addressing issues with your NPD parent. Evaluating which avenue you take will create a fuller opportunity to surface issues of loss, identify fears, and understand more clearly where old patterns keep you stuck.

For some of us, the circumstances of expressing our feelings to our NPD parent(s) may not be a viable one. Sometimes the stakes are too high in terms of potential for further emotional abuse, financial retaliation, or being cut off from the NPD parent and/or other family members. However, we are far more likely to be resistant due to our reluctance to encounter the intensity of our feelings. We are simply afraid to face the powerful feelings and emotions associated with taking such a bold step.

In addition, you may easily confuse the goal of initiating fuller discussion about your feelings with the goal of trying to change your NPD parent in some significant way. In terms of this first level of work, you may have difficulty understanding that *changing your NPD parent is not the goal.* The goal is to change your own behavior in the presence of your NPD parent, which will lead to empowerment and repair of your self-esteem.

As you initiate the opportunity to have this discussion (which includes setting boundaries) with your NPD parent, you are undertaking a powerful healing step, a process often termed "re-parenting." In other words, *you are creating a corrective emotional experience for yourself by standing up for the small child you once were as you share your feelings in the presence of your parent.* I emphasize that this is the primary reason for committing to this hard work.

By contrast, *the second level of work with your NPD parent is done to reshape your parent's toxic behavior through the use of assertiveness tools.* The goal here is not to "fix" your NPD parent but, instead, to limit the degree of his or her inappropriate behavior in your presence. In short, you will be walking the fine line between asserting your needs and feelings—while resisting the trap of vengeful dumping or angry ventilation.

Preparing for this discussion involves encountering the fears we had as a child when we were once faced with the forceful, imposing NPD parent who threatened us with disapproval, indifference, humiliation, painful punishment, removal of love, or abandonment. Finally, you may also fear hurting your NPD parent by threatening the fragile woundedness in her—a compassion that has played an additional role in holding you hostage to the old behavior patterns. Naturally, these fears lie at the heart of your reluctance to address your feelings openly because these same fears kept you bound to the will of your NPD parent in childhood. Consequently, you must carefully and fully prepare yourself for these interventions.

Writing a letter to your NPD parent (whether you decide to send it or not) is a helpful tool and one that is advocated by many therapists and self-help books. Carefully articulating your feelings first on paper so that you can sort through the big picture is an effective form of mental and emotional rehearsal. This process facilitates more opportunity to work through repressed feelings even when you think you have already done this work.

If you decide to send your letter, you are able to express a balanced perspective of the issues and feelings that you want to convey, both the positives and negatives—your love and your anger. You also avoid the trap of expressing only the painful feelings (although in some cases positive feelings are difficult or even impossible to discover). A letter also offers the assurance that you will not lose your focus and get caught up in the routine defensive dance with your NPD parent. Finally, a letter offers some guarantee that your NPD parent will have to give you his undivided attention because he cannot engage you in defensive distractions.

An example of the healing impact of "therapeutic" letters can be seen in the story of a client we will call Paul. Although he had devoted hard work in therapy on the near-obsessive feelings of anger he felt towards his NPD father, he had to acknowledge that he was unable to let go and move forward with the rest of his life. His father, who had literally abandoned him as a teenager to many difficult circumstances, lived near-by and treated him as if he did not exist. After considerable work in therapy, it became clear to me that Paul would not be able to get beyond the anger that possessed him until he confronted these feelings in some concrete form with his father.

When I suggested to him that he begin to work on a letter to his father, Paul resisted mightily. With further prodding on my part, he reluctantly began to put his feelings on paper, although he remained adamant that he would never send the letter. In Paul's case, I remained supportive of his final decision but stated my belief that his reluctance to confront his feelings directly with his NPD father was playing a role in his emotional stalemate. Eventually, Paul came into therapy one day and informed me that he had finally decided to send his letter. Over the next several sessions he reported that he had indeed experienced a dramatic release from the grip of his anger and rage almost as soon as he had put the letter in the box!

If you decide to initiate a discussion face to face with your NPD parent, you will want to address your thoughts, one on one, regardless of the context—discussion or letter. A common error is to engage in these discussions with both parents simultaneously. This undermines the process primarily by blurring the boundaries of individuals and not allowing for more effective direct communication.

The final goal of sharing your feelings openly with your NPD parent is to discover and/or validate the depth of your parent's issues of narcissistic wounding. As you bring the full maturity of your experience to the problems with this parent, you will witness how much he or she is willing and able to engage in the process of understanding you as a separate person. If your parent shows some ability to grasp the messages you are conveying, you have uncovered the fact that he has some capacity for true self-reflection and change.

On the other hand, if your parent reveals that she is incapable of understanding what you are saying, or demonstrates an inability to remember from one day to the next, you are able to discover the depth of her limitations. In this case, you achieve greater awareness and validation of what your history has been. This anchoring of your reality will also assist you to fully mourn the losses with your NPD parent and let go of unconscious expectations and hopes for change. A more mature and peaceful acceptance of yourself and your NPD parent is now possible.

A client we will call Nancy realized as she began this process that she had always felt responsible for her mother's feelings, regardless of the circumstance or situation. She also began to recognize that her mother's narcissism had been the significant dynamic instilling these feelings in her. When she initiated a dialogue process with her mother to discuss these issues, she surfaced the painful defenses surrounding her mother's narcissism. Painful and difficult as these encounters were, she was able to validate her perceptions and reject the unconscious role that had been necessary to survive childhood. She could now fully recognize the depth of her sadness and mourn the losses she had endured as a child. This final phase of healing was more powerful than any other emotional work she had done previously because it integrated her intellectual awareness to a deeper understanding of her feelings.

Finally, you will want to address the second level of work (reshaping your parent's toxic behaviors) with your NPD parent if he or she is still living, and you have an ongoing relationship with him or her. Also, as mentioned before, you may have decided that the first level of work (the decision to have a fuller discussion about your feelings with your NPD parent) may not be a viable one. Regardless of your choice about this first level of work, you will want to practice assertiveness skills so that you can limit your NPD parent's more hurtful and antagonistic behavior patterns, such as the devaluing behaviors or the double-bind messages discussed in chapter three.

This stage of work also pushes us to face our rationalizations that say there is no point to embark on this venture because our NPD parent(s) will never change. We must confront the paper tiger of our NPD parent's defenses so that we can see past the illusion—the illusion that keeps us stuck and unable to assert our own rights in the relationship.

Even when a narcissistic parent demonstrates the inability for insight, he is capable of learning (over time) that the ground rules for interacting with you have changed. He is able to learn that he must curb his inappropriate behaviors. In other words, he may not truly "get it" (regarding your feelings), but he will begin to respond to your new limits with some measure of restraint. When you remain consistent and follow through with your stated consequences regarding those behaviors you have targeted for change, you will command the respect that must be fought for with the narcissist. As you begin the necessary process of setting limits, boundaries, and new rules that insist on reciprocal respect, you can reliably predict that you will initially be met with a defensive outrage such as a martyr-like "How could you?" or a self-righteous "How dare you?"

The need to anticipate your NPD parent's "change-back" responses requires preparation; in the beginning, you can reliably count on this dynamic as part of the process. *"Change-back" responses are the defensive escalation of manipulative behaviors intended to prevent you from changing your former role and/or behavior patterns.* These reactions on the part of your NPD parent are not only predictable but also impressively forceful and intense. You, like Dorothy, are facing the Great Oz with all the terror and uncertainty so dramatically illustrated in the story. At first you may be met with a searing assault intended to produce guilt, anger, or self-doubt. Perhaps you are shunned as your NPD parent sulks or ignores you in family interactions. But, don't give up! Hold your own by maintaining consistency with your new behaviors and do not "take the bait" by reacting to your NPD parent's defenses. You will discover that your NPD parent will eventually accommodate to the required changes. The change-back dynamic is another reason that you need to prepare yourself so that you can weather the storm of your NPD parent's escalating threats.

An example of this "change-back" dynamic can be seen in the following scenario. A woman named Jessie began to address her mother's narcissistic behaviors in small interventions, initially having short (prescheduled) discussions with her. During these discussions Jessie described the specific behaviors that she felt were critical (on her mother's part). Jessie then expressed how she felt when her mother behaved this way. She concluded these dialogues by telling her mother that her goal was to have a positive relationship with her, yet also warned her that she would no longer tolerate these critical behaviors and would end her visits and phone calls if her mother repeated them.

Jessie had wisely anticipated her mother's defensive maneuvers and was ready to respond non-defensively through comments such as, "I'm sorry you're hearing me that way; that's not what I'm saying," and "I do love you, but I can't tolerate these frequent criticisms and comparisons," etc. As a result, her conversations with her mother improved and her mother's attitude became more respectful.

A client, named Denise, began to anticipate her mother's defensive reactions as she envisioned herself asserting some new limits. "If I tell my mother that I don't want to see her every week, she will tell me that she always took care of *her* mother and wasn't even allowed to learn to drive. I guess I would tell her that it was her choice if she didn't learn to drive. She should have learned how to drive." As we rehearsed her intervention Denise began to see how she was already getting caught in a distracting issue (her mother not learning to drive). Instead of allowing her mother to distract her from the topic, she rehearsed staying focused on the issue (her need for more flexibility in visiting her mother).

Instead of debating and defending herself, Denise chose to validate her mother's loss, but then return the focus to their own relationship. For instance, she might say, "Mom, I can certainly understand how difficult it must have been with your own mother, and you may have a lot of feelings about that. However, I am not willing to settle for these expectations in *our* relationship." Don't get caught up in the debate about some connecting but different issue. *As you maintain the focus on the narcissistic demands and behaviors you intend to set limits on, you won't fall into the trap* of who's right, who's wrong, who's hurt, who isn't. In this case, Denise needed to limit her mother's expectation (and implicit demand) that she visit her weekly without fail, regardless of Denise's needs. Staying focused on the issue allowed her to assert her rights and her intention to change this pattern (giving her mother a specific description of this change).

You can expect your NPD parent to defensively engage you in the either/or debate. By now, you have learned not to take the bait. You can respond to these maneuvers by indicating that you understand his feelings and then calmly, but firmly, reassert the focus of discussion. Address the situation at hand, remind him of the behaviors you are addressing, and communicate what you expect him to remember about that. Every time you practice these assertive behaviors with your NPD parent, you are developing greater awareness of yourself and your feelings, as well as recognizing the important distinctions between you and your NPD parent.

With the more overt type of narcissistic parent, you may receive the competitive taunt. For instance, an NPD father might attempt to deflect the issues at hand by ridiculing his son, saying he just can't "take the heat" and taunting him to engage in the battle of "who's better." In this dynamic, the son needs to confront the narcissistic grandiosity for what it is and calmly opt out of the competition, asserting his right to be heard on the topic he is addressing.

You can see that learning basic assertiveness skills is an integral part of this process. Anticipating your NPD parent's maneuvers in advance will help you to resist reacting to them in the way that you have done so many times in the past. As you learn to deal assertively with your NPD parent, you will develop a profound new sense of self-esteem. Your growth will gain momentum through these efforts, and you will find that the benefits expand to many other areas of your life as well.

At this point, you also need to recognize the insidiously subtle, but potent forces of your parent's narcissistic defenses. When you can recognize the many traps of these dynamics, you can keep them in check or neutralize them as you encounter them. As I mentioned in chapter three, the primary defense on the part of the narcissistic parent or individual involves the blurring and usurping of boundaries in any given relationship. This is magnified to the extreme in the relationship between the NPD parent and his child. In a nutshell, this is the origin and perpetuation of all your pain in your relationship with your NPD parent. Depending on the severity of the narcissism, your parent may be completely incapable of recognizing the separate boundary of "you," and, therefore, incapable of giving you any consensual validation of your own reality.

Connected to this usurping of boundaries are a number of unconscious behaviors on the part of the narcissistic person that are extremely effective at undermining your ability to feel confident in yourself or remain focused on your goals or plans. Two of the most disturbing dynamics are those we talked about in chapter three, the double message/double bind, and the simple but effective manipulation of a tenaciously persistent repetition of criticism.

In Richard Restak's enlightening and comprehensive book on character disorders, *The Self Seekers*, he gives special attention to these dynamics. Under the section heading, "Lessons in How to Drive Another Person Really Crazy," he gives vivid examples of how difficult it can be for even the most "healthy" and confident individual to withstand the repetitively expressed doubts or criticisms of another individual, particularly someone close. In one example, Restak cites a vignette borrowed from Harold Serles, an esteemed expert on character disorders, about a man who persistently casts doubts on his sister-in-law's mental stability.

> "In discussions with her, he repeatedly refers to her behavior with comments which suggest that her behavior is inconsistent and her personality more than slightly unstable. Since everyone, on occasion, expresses feelings which are inconsistent with previous declarations, it's not too difficult to find and focus in on examples of seeming contradictions. Indeed, if this process is continued beyond a certain point, an individual's self-evaluation becomes threatened. Faced with the force of another person's expression of doubt concerning our adjustment, we gradually begin to suspect that we are not adjusted at all, but only pretending at adjustment. Our confoundment can be further increased if the attacker reinterprets past adjustment as proof of our unwillingness to face squarely certain problems, which, unresolved, have stimulated deliberate efforts on our part to *appear* adjusted. Thus, we are accused simultaneously of being adjusted and not being adjusted."

Here, also, we begin to see the insidious dynamic of the double message in addition to the persistent negative criticisms. As Restak points out, eventually we will begin to respond to the "snowball effect in which disquietude rapidly turns into panic and a painful inner terror that there might be some nugget of truth" as we encounter another person's relentlessly restated accusations. At least remembering this simple fact can help us overcome a sense of additional failure or weakness as we head towards self-doubt or feel insecure when exposed to these behaviors.

All too often I hear clients express that something is wrong with them since, after all, they have such insecure feelings when interacting with their NPD parent. Even when we know that these messages are false, the mere experience of receiving repetitive hits on the same spot, in the same manner, will create an insidious and profoundly negative impact on our sense of well-being. Therefore, we must recognize the toxic nature of these repeating messages and work to limit our exposure to them by confronting and demanding that they stop or by leaving or ending conversations when they occur.

Equally powerful and perhaps more difficult to identify is the maddening dynamic of the double message. While all of us are capable of being inconsistent at times, the narcissistically wounded individual has a much more profound and unconscious experience of being "split" within himself. He will, therefore, have a tendency to project this split self onto others and then criticize others for not responding to one of the two opposite messages. The end result of this dynamic is the double bind or no-win situation since you cannot possibly respond adequately to two messages in direct opposition to one another. Restak describes this experience as follows:

> "Other examples of similar discrepancies between our self-evaluation and another person's evaluation of us include the deliberate creation of ambiguous situations in which we are left in doubt about how to respond. For instance, a person may speak or act in a sexually provocative manner within a setting where sexual interaction is impossible. Or, he may alternate expressions of profound seriousness with playful humor. In this way, we are

simultaneously informed that we are both important enough to merit being "taken seriously" and yet ridiculous enough to be the butt of humorous hostility.

Another variation involves the retention of a single emotional tone when discussing both serious and trivial matters. Both of these techniques aim at the confusion and bewilderment of another person's sense of self. Am I *really* the person I consider myself to be or, instead, a kind of humorous figure, a distorted and fragmented self which is both serious and comic, sane and insane, a creature of certitude and yet, someone who is irresolute and incomplete?"

Perhaps a universal double message that the NPD parent communicates is an insistent expectation that you measure up to his standards of perfection while also stating his belief that you are too incompetent to achieve these standards. Communicating with the narcissistic parent involves a confusing mixture of these types of painful interactions. Your first clue that this dynamic is at play will be your feelings of increased anxiety or confusion as you interact with the NPD parent. Sometimes you will only see the double bind after you have been caught in the trap and feel the anger or (at times) rage that results from the set-up. The ability to begin calling your parent out from hiding on these patterns will again allow you to validate your own reality and take assertive steps towards self-care in the presence of your parent.

Ultimately, your choices about which interventions you are willing to work on with your NPD parent are the result of the powerful healing work you have done in the safer setting of therapy. A middle-aged woman I will call Colleen had pursued several therapies and accomplished a lot of healing in her adult life. Colleen once told me, "You know, even though my father is a frail, withered little man in his eighties, and I am a strong, younger adult, I always feel like a terrified little girl when I am in his presence."

She had developed many internal and external supports that enabled her to have short visits with her father. She had worked in therapy to learn assertiveness skills for setting limits on his verbal abuse and worked hard with mental and emotional rehearsal to hold her own when she was in his presence. You may be wondering why she didn't just cut him loose and forget about him if he was that abusive! The response to this is that the goal you choose for the ongoing relationship with your NPD parent is a uniquely personal and individual one.

If you have experienced abuse or neglect with an NPD parent, you have probably struggled with your need to maintain some kind of relationship with this parent, despite your recognition of the limitations and inability for this parent to provide love and acceptance. This is a natural and common need and one that must be honored and respected. The important issue in making this choice is to develop the skills that allow this goal to be a healthy one.

While Colleen had a devastating history of abuse, she had a deep need to sustain her relationship with her father as a way of defining herself as different from her father. By maintaining a self-assertive, self-caring stance in his presence, she was able to develop a healthy experience of self, one deserving of respect and love. She also knew she could not achieve the fulfillment of reciprocal love in her relationship with her father due to his complete inability for empathy or consideration of another person.

However, her choice to maintain a relationship with her NPD father enabled her to feel a deep sense of meaning in her refusal to give in to the feelings of hatred she had so relentlessly experienced in the form of her father's negative projections. This did not mean that she had not worked through her feelings of rage, hurt, and sadness. She had, in fact, accomplished significant healing regarding these feelings. In the last phase of Colleen's healing work, her most meaningful choice was to treat her father respectfully and demand respect from him. Whatever the choice you decide upon for your ongoing relationship, it is vital that you enter into the process of confronting and setting limits on the narcissistic demands and manipulations of your NPD parent(s).

For most of us there is an intense dilemma surrounding our ability to know if the choices we have made about our lives are those of our own or those of our NPD parent(s). For instance, we may be unable to know if the career we have chosen is truly the one we want, or if we chose it to please or displease our NPD parent. As mentioned in chapter two, like the son in the film *Shine,* we may be haunted by our uncertainty about what we really want. The musician in *Shine* had to discover his desire and ability to claim his music for himself, a choice that required him to separate from his father. Here again, we return to the challenge that the only way out of our dilemma is to test, probe, and discover our true feelings.

The pervasive anxiety and fear that is often experienced as we re-evaluate our choices about our lives is probably a universally shared experience. You may say to yourself, "I don't know what I really want. I don't know what really makes me happy. And besides, I can't stand the anxiety. Maybe living with the 'shoulds' isn't so bad. After all, at least it makes the anxiety go away." Each time your feelings of fear surface, it can be your opportunity to confront the unacknowledged feelings of anger, hurt, and sorrow.

In addition to working through fears in therapy, you must seek out coaches or mentors who can support you as you discover your strengths and weaknesses, take effective steps towards initial goals, and make "course corrections" as you recognize what you really want. In addition, you will notice that your fears diminish over time as you employ new strategies and behaviors that point you in the direction of your goals. With every courageous new effort, you shatter the engrained messages of your NPD parent(s) that are internalized. Primarily, you are facing head on the implied threat behind the "shoulds" of your parent's "Do as I say or else!" This "or else" might have meant loss of love, punishment, humiliation, guilt, or any number of crushing emotional experiences when you thought of disobeying their expectations.

Of course, as your readiness to implement your action plan is now fully developed, you can still expect to face old ghosts and strong fears. Eventually, as you continue to push through these fears, testing out old and new choices, you will discover the choices that are the truest reflections of your authentic self. The profound satisfaction, clarity, and fulfillment that you gain are the long-awaited rewards. In the end, you will discover the many gifts and talents of your own natural being. Like the discoveries of Dorothy, Tin Man, Scarecrow, and Lion, they lie deep within and can only be found as we penetrate our deepest illusions and fears.

Coping with the Dying NPD Parent

The narcissist who has spent his life unable and perhaps unwilling to reflect on himself and his life beyond his surface pursuits, will generally find death terrifying. Since the heart of this disorder is the inability to recognize the self as having limits and fallibility, death is the ultimate confrontation of our mortality—a reality far too overwhelming for the narcissist to contemplate. Consequently, the NPD individual generally copes with his own impending death through an elaborate set of denial, avoidance, and manipulation strategies. All the defenses of the NPD person are now intensified towards a single focus, the maddening and exasperating dilemma of the double bind.

The double bind for the hospital or hospice staff is most likely the ultimate no-win situation with ominous possibilities. Hospice staff comprises individuals who have the admirable and challenging job of ministering to the dying patient and his family, a job few people could imagine themselves doing day in and day out. These individuals are truly heroic in their courage and empathy as they enter into the life of a person or family at its toughest point, that of saying goodbye.

With the NPD individual, hospice staff will generally experience one of two extremes: they might be blocked at every juncture when they try to assist, or they may find themselves overwhelmed by the unrelenting neediness and demands of the NPD patient. In some cases, the NPD patient may simply refuse to allow any hospice involvement. In situations like this, you as a family member are now faced with the challenging burden of putting your entire life on hold in order to take on this role. You may also be simultaneously placed at the center of the family conflict and finger pointing regarding who is to blame for the mounting problems of your NPD mom or dad's difficult dying process.

Eventually, you may find yourself finding fault and becoming angry with the doctors or hospice workers for not complying with the wishes of your NPD parent, or not taking good care of your NPD parent. Similarly, the hospice staff may find themselves on the defensive and become more concerned that they are being targeted for a setup.

We can see how confusing and difficult the situation is for hospital personnel to know how to care for a patient who communicates a confusing pattern of double messages. Their position becomes even more trying as they simultaneously juggle the legal implications of their judgments, especially under pressure. Fundamentally, to be called in to do a job and then not be allowed to do it is exasperating.

If family members and medical staff do not have effective communication surrounding the NPD person's care, the two camps will be at odds, increasingly falling into the trap of the distraction and chaos-producing behaviors of the NPD patient. The final phase of the NPD parent is often a constantly changing labyrinth of chaos and confusion contrasted by your intense hope and effort to have some quality life or quality relationship. Even in the process of the Last Will and Testament of the NPD person, you will often find bitter pills to swallow.

The story of a colleague's NPD grandmother painfully illustrates an example of this. My friend's NPD grandmother had enjoyed the family's long-standing admiration and envy of her unique ability to prepare an ethnic dish, which was a family favorite. No one could ever persuade her to reveal her secret recipe. The moment of suspense reached its height at the time of her impending death. With a sense of sad resignation and curiosity, my friend wondered whether or not her grandmother would place more importance on remaining the single person who could cook such a delight or, instead, share the recipe as something she could be remembered by to succeeding generations.

In the end, the grandmother played out the double message with perfection. As she made ceremony of the fact that she had put her secret recipe into her Will, the family members offered gratitude and appreciation for her gift. Following her death, when family members prepared the dish, they discovered the recipe was completely wrong! Perhaps you might think she simply made a mistake; after all, she had probably never written it down before. On the other hand, perhaps she played out the double bind to the bittersweet end—gaining the recognition for giving away her recipe while remaining the sole person who would ever prepare it.

These last scenarios from the end phase of the NPD parent's life are inevitably an extension and often a magnification of the overall style of defenses that your parent has been demonstrating all your life. If the NPD parent has shown some signs of growth and change through the aging process, chances are the dying process will include some ability on his part for cooperation and acceptance. When this is possible, an adult child may experience meaningful moments of softer connection with the NPD parent that can ultimately become cherished memories.

On the other hand, the dying experience will often be filled with difficult and impossible stalemates creating untold stress for family members. In addition, the NPD parent can be the instigator of painful dissension within the family that may result in permanently ostracizing or disowning certain members. Because he has been so effective at artfully dividing and conquering family members one at a time, he may even come through smelling like the proverbial "rose," never identified as the catalyst of all the family strife.

To prepare, and possibly protect yourself from the potential pain and frustration throughout this experience, refer to the following three strategies. You will find them to be your most helpful coping skills.

- Self-care—Allow yourself to utilize resources and supports that alleviate stress and bring you pleasure. You may need to regularly brainstorm (tap into other people's experience for ideas) to think of new ways to gain relief and find opportunities for pleasure separate from and perhaps at times with your NPD parent.

- Boundary Setting—Give regular reminders to the NPD parent of what you can and can't do regarding his/her care. Also include gentle but firm pushes to encourage him/her to (at times insist that he/she) do those things that he/she can do independently.

- Communication—Remember, it is not possible to have too much information from and direct communication with the doctors, as well as other family members. When in doubt, ask!

Your commitment to your own care (that may seem a secondary concern in a crisis) will greatly benefit you in the long run, since you cannot know what you will encounter during your parent(s)' dying process. The quality of your time together will reflect your ability to take care of yourself alongside your NPD parent. The peace of mind alone that these efforts bring is well worthwhile.

CHAPTER FIVE SUMMARY

The painful nature of a psychological symptom can be our greatest ally when we are willing to learn the message it is trying to convey from deep within the psyche. Growing up with an NPD parent assures us that we have encountered wounding to the self and are in need of healing. However, our defenses of denial, repression, projection, introjection, and many others were developed along the path to adulthood, numbing the feelings and creating false beliefs about who we are. Eventually, the distress we feel from our symptoms will help us recognize that these defenses are now sabotaging our lives preventing the fulfillment of intimacy and other goals. Indeed, most of us require the painful grip of a symptom before we are willing to look within and rediscover our inherent ability to know our true feelings.

Because healing requires the help of a safe person who can provide the gentle push to face our inner selves, working with a skilled therapist is often the most effective way to accomplish genuine healing and lasting change. In this process, we inevitably face the fears of our childhood—fear that our feelings will overwhelm us causing permanent harm. This childhood fear becomes the driving force behind our defenses, perpetuating our avoidance, and fueling the inscrutable nature of our symptoms.

At this juncture we also confront the indoctrination that prohibits us from facing those times when our parents did indeed disappoint and wound our need for love. We sidestep the issue with the worn out refrain that we don't want to "cast blame" or "use our parents as an excuse" for our own failings. Yet we pay for this pseudo understanding with enslavement to our defenses—defenses that keep us numb to our feelings, unable to develop empathy for the self. We must face our feelings head on if we are to develop genuine compassion and forgiveness for the limitations of our parents and the limitations in ourselves.

As we acknowledge the truth of our history, we need to grieve the losses, whether in the form of hurt, betrayal, neglect, rejection, or abandonment. Slowly we recognize the resilience and strength that comes from the ability to know and empathize with all of our feelings. Hurt, anger, loneliness, and fear no longer overwhelm us, but exist as part of the rich terrain in our travels through life.

The last phase of healing is the empowerment stage. Now we must anchor our progress in behavior change that demonstrates an ability to "re-parent" the child we once were, standing up for our thoughts and feelings and setting limits on the NPD parent (if living). Preparation and rehearsal in therapy will help with the important goals of:

- Identifying and fully expressing your feelings associated with your NPD parent(s') hurtful behaviors, both past and present (whether in person or only in therapy).

- Developing assertiveness and boundary setting skills that reshape the NPD parent(s') behaviors—behaviors that require greater respect on the part of your NPD parent for your thoughts, feelings, and choices.

As you recognize the unique dynamics of your NPD parent(s)' defensive manipulations, you can counter them with effective limit setting strategies that will improve the quality of your interactions, regardless of change on the part of your NPD parent(s). Another benefit is the powerful healing of your self-esteem—one that impacts many other areas of your life.

Finally, these efforts will help you cope with the ending phase of your NPD parent's life. Often the defenses of the NPD parent escalate in the dying process (either in facing his/her own death or the death of his/her partner). Your increased ability for self-care, boundary setting, and communication will allow you to maximize the possibility of quality time and avoid the pitfalls of the "emotional hostage" trap. Self-care, boundary setting, and communication are the primary means that will help you avoid regret or resentment in the aftermath of your NPD parent(s)' death, or the death of your codependent parent.

If He Only Had a Heart

The Intimate Love Relationship

My heart compels me to him
Ah, could I touch and hold him
And kiss him as I wanted
With his kisses I could perish
Oh, could I perish with his kiss
Oh, could I kiss him as I wanted

My peace is gone
My heart is heavy
I can find it never, nevermore
If I cannot have him

—Franz Schubert, paraphrased excerpt from
the "*Spinning Song*," Goethe's *Faust*

This song of "fatal attraction" is the expression of Margeurite's desperate love for Faust, who has hypnotized her with his newly acquired powers of irresistible beauty and strength. The age-old wisdom in the story of *Faust* demonstrates the extremities of unhealthy narcissism on both sides of the coin, the narcissist and the narcissist's partner.

Faust, who makes a pact with the devil for the unlimited powers of earthly life, money, influence, and youth, is perhaps a disturbing analogy to the insidious defenses that envelope the narcissist as he pursues his grandiose standards, relentlessly chasing a false self that will never bring him satisfaction. However, the remarkable insights revealed in the "Spinning Song" demonstrate Schubert's recognition that Margeurite, like Faust, has also compromised her very soul. Her words, "My peace is gone forever," reveal her understanding that she is subjugating her own self (symbolized by her inner peace) to the object of her love. Similar to Faust, she wishes to make her moment of choice disappear in a puff of smoke, like a magic trick, pretending that she has not really chosen. She cannot face her abdication, and the illusory moment of self-deception occurs while she mournfully grieves the loss of her "peace" as a *fait accompli*. In her lovesick torment, she submits to her temptation and commits her fate to the will of Faust.

The intoxicating power of total infatuation is a tragic seduction that all of us have experienced in one way or another. On the one hand, we sense when we are infatuated that we are succumbing to an illusion; on the other hand, our fervor is so compelling that we don't seem to care about the price we will pay. What better analogy than Margeurite's love for Faust to illustrate the consuming intoxication we feel when pursued by the narcissist as he entices us into his world of the extraordinary?

Indeed, Faust is no ordinary man, and his larger-than-life countenance is based on something Margeurite could never imagine. She does not know that Faust's allegiance lies elsewhere. Faust has sworn his soul for his desires just as the narcissist is enslaved to a grandiose false self. In a complementary fashion, the codependent partner sacrifices her allegiance to her own self for her allegiance to the grandiose self of her partner, never realizing the falseness that underlies such a bond. Similar to Margeurite, we become transformed and transfixed by the experience of entering into such a godlike world.

The seduction and persuasiveness of the narcissist is a force that is aptly portrayed by Faust as he pursues Margeurite. Often the narcissistic individual is initially the pursuer in romantic relationships. Before receiving his attentions, you may not have felt drawn to him. However, once he devotes himself to the single-minded purpose of attaining your love, he can quite literally sweep you off your feet or outlast any reservations you may have about the relationship. It is as if you succumb to his ardor because of the sheer force and unrelenting nature of his will, a force that is a hallmark of his narcissism.

If we have experienced certain types of wounding in childhood, we are more vulnerable to this type of attraction—the attraction to the grandiose self of the narcissistic individual. *Similar to the narcissist, we seek a substitute to compensate for our feelings of inadequacy. However, unlike the narcissist, we find this substitute through our attachment to the grandiose self in someone else.* If you are the codependent in this relationship, you are on the opposite side of the coin, gaining your sense of self through your ability to support and be an indispensable part of another person's world. Your NPD partner achieves what he so intensely craves, your devoted admiration as well as his need to idealize your own admirable qualities (making you a worthy mirror of his grandiose self). As the codependent partner, you also achieve the perfect love object, *someone who inspires and elevates your compulsion to nurture—a partner who gives purpose to your mission to give.*

At first, this arrangement appears to be made in heaven with such mutual and compatible desires. You may be quite blissful in the glow of shared adoration and apparent love for a period of time. Unfortunately, this euphoria is usually a fleeting experience before the first disillusionment dashes the love like glass shattering on stone. Your NPD partner's disillusionment is typically ushered in by his first recognition of your imperfection as a human being. On an unconscious level he feels the pressure of greater intimacy as you express your desire for an ongoing emotional connection with him. You may feel that the desire for a deeper connection is a natural extension of the process of living life together day by day.

However, the intimacy of emotional sharing is not within your NPD partner's comfort zone because he is cut off from his true feelings, defined instead by his all-consuming drive to support a grandiose persona or purpose. You may feel a terrible shock as you see the dark side of your partner's defenses and his need to flee from the threat of intimacy. He may escape into his unending work responsibilities, social distractions, or insatiable needs for "playing hard." He will also seek reasons to justify these escapes with regular rebukes of your "neediness" and/or your unrealistic or unfair expectations.

In general, your NPD partner finds fault with you as he becomes frustrated and pressured by your "need" of him. His criticism and complaints may now trigger deep feelings of inadequacy in you and activate your own unconscious struggle for reassurance that you are worthy of love. For a time, you each fortify your defense strategies—your NPD partner demands more, and you sacrifice more as you try harder to please him. Your quarrels and escalating fights are most likely generating underlying feelings of frustration, suspicion, fear, and inadequacy in both of you. Here in the inner sanctum of your intimate relationship, the painful erosion of love is hidden from the outside world, family, and friends.

If you are in pain because you are discovering that your partner has a number of the narcissistic traits we have discussed, you are probably in one of two stages:

- The first stage is one of shock, hurt, and confusion about your partner's temper or his/her cold detachment alongside the unexpected barrage of criticisms vented towards you. You are undoubtedly soul searching and appealing to your partner to understand what has brought about such hurtful and demeaning treatment.

- The second stage is one of accommodation. In this stage you have learned to negotiate your way around the land mines of his/her temper and critical attacks by avoiding any interaction and communication that you fear will cause conflict. Perhaps the tempest of these defensive behaviors have calmed down because you have "backed off" and lowered your expectations of this relationship considerably.

By the time you are in the second stage, her defenses have firmly established who is in control in your relationship, and the whole experience has left you wondering where things went wrong and how to make them right. You probably are not sure how you feel about her and vacillate between an intense longing to recapture the early love and your growing resentment that the relationship has become so one-sided and hurtful.

You may remember from chapter two that the narcissist's primary defenses revolve around her absorption and allegiance to her grandiose self, which is always based on a belief that she is uniquely special and exceptional regardless of the persona she manifests. Because her defenses prevent much awareness of her deeper feelings or the feelings of others, at times you are incredulous that she seems so oblivious to your increasing hurt and estrangement from her. Only when you threaten to rock the boat by expressing your unhappiness or you withdraw your usual support do you receive the worst of her defensive anger and sharp criticisms. Your partner's profound denial of the emotional reality of others invariably prevents her from recognizing and/or later remembering your attempts to signal your discouragement and isolation in the relationship.

The opposite and yet equally difficult set of grandiose defenses can occur in the form of your own codependent false self—the role or persona of the caretaker. Again, depending on the severity of narcissistic traits, your codependent defenses can also manifest the full-blown narcissistic personality disorder in the form of the "closet" or covert narcissist. You may remember from chapter two that the covert narcissist is one whose grandiose self is manifested primarily through her role or mission. If you are coping with only a selection of narcissistic traits, you will most likely be the partner who recognizes the imperative to address your personal and/or your relationship issues.

On the codependent side of the relationship coin are the complementary defenses that cause you to abdicate any awareness of your own needs (especially emotional). Therefore, you abandon your responsibility to assert these needs as equal to those of your partner's in the relationship. You may vacillate between a pattern of conceding your thoughts and feelings to those of your partner while intermittently releasing your frustration and hurt through intense emotional outbursts of hurt and anger. These episodes are often followed by feelings of despair and humiliation that your NPD partner characterizes you as hysterical, over-reactive, or crazy. Perhaps you also buy into this notion about your feelings after many exhausting scenes of escalated fighting.

If you are the male partner to the NPD woman, your efforts to express your dissatisfaction in the relationship may be even less apparent because your coping strategies involve a pattern of shutting your NPD partner out and remaining passive to her numerous and often unreasonable demands.

Eventually, regardless of gender differences and the endless variation of psychological defense strategies, you may become vulnerable to escaping into alcohol, an affair, or any number of potential addictions. In my private practice in an affluent community, I frequently see the codependent partner escaping into an obsessive absorption with the standards and image of a life with quality and class. The following chart provides the framework of the complementary defenses that lead to such a painful stagnation in the relationship.

True Self

We are born with the capacity to experience and express our authentic self.

As childhood unfolds, the child will experience some wounding or lack of support for his or her developmental needs because of the unresolved emotional issues of the parents or primary caretakers. Depending on the *type* of childhood wounding, the child will be directed towards one of two primary defensive styles to survive this wounding.

(continued)

Childhood Wounding

The type of wounding will determine one of two general directions the child will take.

The individual survives this wounding through the...	The individual survives this wounding through the...
Codependent's false self	**Narcissist's false self**
Grandiose nurturer/caretaker	● Grandiose achiever, or unique persona—possessor of special talent or status
Focused on the feelings and needs of others	● Focused on the feelings and needs of self
Gifts of empathy, insight and generosity	● Gifts of leadership and achievement
Strength—has gift of inner wisdom and truth, awareness of the importance of empathy and emotional connectedness	● Strength—ability to project his/her vision into the world, recruit others into this vision
Limitation—cannot take a stand for his/her own truth, cannot assert feelings and needs	● Limitation—cannot identify feelings to know his/her inner truth, cannot empathize with the feelings of others
Invests trust and resources too easily	● Suspicious of others; withholds resources
Demands of others	**Demands of others**
Approval	● Admiration
Ability to make others happy	● Conformity
Avoidance of conflict	● Place his/her needs first
Fear Driven	**Anger Driven**
Represses feelings of anger, unworthiness, fear of abandonment	● Represses feelings of hurt, inadequacy, and fear of humiliation

Over time, the primary feelings that you as the codependent partner typically experience in these relationships are:

- Hurt and frustration because your partner regularly minimizes your need for emotional intimacy in the relationship and becomes defensive and critical.

- Self-doubt about the legitimacy of your emotional needs.

- Devalued and demeaned if you are viewed by him or her as "less than"—less competent, less smart, less objective, less important, and so on.

- A growing dread that your partner simply doesn't "get it" about you (understand your feelings) coupled with an uncertainty about who is responsible—you, for not communicating clearly—or him/her, for being unable to comprehend.

- Resignation that causes you to give up expressing your opinions, needs, or feelings because the resulting conflict isn't worth it.

- Isolation and despair about the lack of emotional intimacy.

- Abandonment whenever you recognize that you have legitimate reason to expect his/her support.

The weight of these accumulating feelings within the relationship will eventually generate some sort of crisis for you as the codependent in the relationship. From my experience working with couples, I have noticed a commonly shared pattern in the process of getting to the crisis point that motivates the codependent to seek help or to finally take a proactive stance in her relationship.

Your narcissistic partner's more obvious and concrete wounding pattern is his habitual defensive anger that causes him to devalue you in some way. *The less tangible yet equally wounding behavior is your NPD partner's lack of empathy and support for your emotional needs.* This latter pattern of empathic failure can be quite subtle when committed in the routine of everyday life, but far more wounding when you experience an event that brings this trait to the forefront. As the codependent partner in the relationship, the pain of significant emotional abandonment is generally the wake-up call that catalyzes your emotional crisis in the relationship. In other words, the "sin of omission" on the part of the NPD partner is more often the hurt that creates a deep and profound turning point for you in your feelings towards your NPD partner.

One day, a client I will call Laura came into therapy with many of these difficulties. At first hesitant and perhaps fearful of revealing her inner feelings of dissatisfaction about her marriage, she could only make indirect references to her numb and empty feelings. Then, with an almost knee-jerk reaction she would blame herself for her discontent, citing the entire list of "good husband" qualities present in her partner. Eventually, as Laura felt safe to explore her feelings more fully, she reflected on the undeniable turning point early in her marriage when her husband began his sullen and abusive behaviors towards her.

As his behaviors escalated into an additional pattern of alcohol abuse, she remembered her own conscious response. She had made an oath to herself that she was stronger and could endure whatever it took until his "demons" (whatever they were) were exorcised. For several years she tolerated his abuse and indifference to her feelings by tenaciously countering his behaviors with efforts on her part to be more loving and more understanding. Eventually, he did indeed begin to settle down. As he resumed more responsible conduct in his life generally, he seemed to regard the whole matter as a phase, simply a bad dream that was now past.

Of course, Laura, who had been nurturing a pattern of tolerant, forgiving passivity, was unable to insist on her need to talk about her feelings. Now that the crisis appeared to have passed, she realized that she had a desperate need to release her anger and hurt and gain an understanding of what had happened. On the occasions when Laura did assert her need to talk, her husband remained adamant in his defensive unwillingness to discuss the past. He would instead aim his criticisms at Laura for "dwelling on the past" when she now had what she wanted.

Laura's most painful loss and disillusionment occurred when she discovered that her husband was unwilling or unable to share feelings of any kind when it came to their relationship, regardless of the context. During his period of abusive self-indulgence, she had withstood his hurtful behavior through a counter-defense of her own by pledging to understand and selflessly support him. Although her codependent tenacity to stand by him, no matter what the cost, had kept them together through this period, she was unprepared for the hurt and anger she felt by his utter lack of empathy or concern for her feelings once the storm had past.

Perhaps these empathic failures on the part of the NPD partner create the crisis point for you because you have been rationalizing your feelings of emotional burnout by telling yourself that your partner will be there for you too when your turn comes. The universal dynamic of the "codependent bargain" is based on the belief that if you give enough, your partner will return the giving, especially at times of importance. When something significant does occur in your life, you may be devastated when your partner demonstrates her inability to support or acknowledge your feelings and needs.

These moments of empathic failure can shatter your confidence in the relationship along with your denial of your partner's limitations to love. The benefit of such painful events is that they become a turning point for you to seek help and support for the long-awaited validation of your thoughts and feelings. Like a survivor stranded on an island, you have been going through life on an emotional starvation diet and denying that you have become so emotionally depleted!

At a similar point, Laura had her most difficult challenge. Because of her own defenses, she was unable to validate or stand up for her right to share her feelings about their relationship. Yet, she was also painfully aware that she felt an inner coldness and, at times, repulsion towards her husband. No matter how hard she tried, she couldn't seem to rekindle her love. Except for feelings of maternal caring, she had no real passion or respect for him. For some time, she had lived in this emotional no-man's land, going through the motions and continuing to tolerate his less severe but often demeaning and controlling behaviors. When she began to suffer from feelings of depression, she sought treatment through an occasional visit to her psychiatrist and antidepressant medication.

Eventually, she took the brave step that her psychiatrist had been recommending and called me to set up an appointment for marital therapy. Her anxious and embarrassed voice on the phone spoke volumes about how much she had been tolerating in her relationship. As I coached her through the steps of how to approach her husband to encourage him to attend their first session together, she reported back in a worried, but hopeful voice that he had agreed to attend. The day of the session, I received a phone call that fully confirmed her initial fears. He had changed his mind at the last minute and became verbally abusive when Laura pressed the matter.

As we continued our discussion, I suggested Laura attend alone. I also encouraged her to tell her husband that she was still attending therapy for herself. Although Laura was not fully conscious of the healing journey she was embarking on, she was taking the first and most important step to empowering herself in the relationship. She was sending him the unequivocal message that she was not happy in the relationship and demonstrating that, despite his unwillingness, she was going about the business of changing for herself.

Often, the most effective signal that will penetrate the NPD partner's denial is your request that he/she attend marital or relationship therapy, and then seeing a relationship therapist yourself (with his/her full knowledge) if he/she fails to join you in taking responsibility for your problems together. Unfortunately, the codependent partner all too often backs down after asserting her wish to attend therapy together and resumes her endless waiting. Other times, she may decide to seek therapy for herself without telling her NPD partner that her reason for attending is principally due to her unhappiness in their relationship. Finally, she may decide to go to therapy, but does so secretively. All of these compromises have significant consequences further down the road. The primary problem is the simple fact that they enable the NPD partner to believe that he or she does not share responsibility for the problems. According to the NPD partner's defenses and perception, the problems that exist are chiefly due to the faults of others, and in this case you!

In addition, you may have your own reasons for failing to indicate that your NPD partner needs to take his or her share of the responsibility for your relationship problems. The first reason is that you buy into her convoluted logic that since YOU are the one who feels unhappy with the relationship, YOU must be the one with the real problem. Or, perhaps you believe her when she convinces you that you can work it out together, despite a pattern of short-lived "good" behavior followed by a return to business as usual. Even if you can get past your own self-doubt about who contributes what to the problems, you may simply be convinced that no one will believe you (even the therapist) when you try to surface the difficulties that she contributes to the relationship.

After all, who knows better than you of your NPD partner's expertise in snowing other people—charming or intimidating them into an impression of how "together," how truly "exceptional" he or she is? Consequently, you may need some time in individual therapy to get your bearings, deal with your own codependency issues, and develop your strength to assert yourself in the relationship. However, *don't lose the precious opportunity to include a warning to your NPD partner, the warning that you are unhappy with the present status of the relationship, and this is one important reason you are seeking help.*

Finally, try to begin your process of healing without shrouding it in the shame of secrecy. I would like to qualify here that taking the step of attending therapy without your partner's knowledge may be better than not seeking help at all. The dilemma, however, is that both you and your therapist can end up in the trap of reinforcing and enabling your belief that you must abdicate your needs in the relationship since you feel it necessary to hide your healing process. I have fallen into this very trap, only to learn that no quality or quantity of therapy could effectively counter the more encompassing message derived from complying with my client's insistence that the therapy needed to be kept a secret from her spouse. This collusion on my part to honor her request and refrain from leaving phone messages or sending mail to her home merely incorporated the therapy into her overriding belief that her needs were not legitimate.

Your primary work involves developing the ability to validate your thoughts, feelings, and needs along with an ability to stand up for yourself in the relationship. This journey requires reconnecting to your feelings and grieving the losses that underlie the defenses that we discussed in chapter five. Your degree of codependency is inevitably the result of childhood wounding experiences, regardless of the injuries that have reinforced these issues in your present relationship.

Individual and relationship therapy, or a combination (with separate therapists) can help you to work on both levels, and gain a sense of perspective. In addition, I find that most of us need some education about the complementary defenses involved in these relationships (severe narcissism and the codependent counterpart) to discover the viability of the potential for healing and growth as a couple.

For codependent individuals working through the stagnating dilemma of their own self-doubt and lack of assertiveness, this journey can take up to two years before significant change is evident. During this time, you are working on your own codependency issues and taking proactive steps that engage your partner to work on his narcissistic traits and/or defenses, regardless of whether he joins you in therapy.

As we return to Laura's story, you may recall that she was struggling mightily between her impulse to accept the status quo of her marriage and her growing inability to tolerate her dissatisfaction and unhappiness. She could no longer deny her feelings of emptiness and isolation despite the appearance of an attractive stable marriage, a fulfilling career, and her belief that she had no *valid* reason to be so unhappy. Laura's tragic dilemma is one that you may identify with if you are discovering that your partner has strong narcissistic traits or the full narcissistic disorder. Laura was recognizing the terrible price that is paid when we give our allegiance to a false self, whether it is our own grandiose false self or that of our partner's. Eventually, we awaken to a life without color, a life that seems so promising on the surface, yet hard and cold inside—a life without vitality and nourishment.

Because Laura had shaped her behavior in the marriage to avoid conflict, she felt reduced to superficial discussions with her husband about work, the outside world, or the routine business of everyday life. The most maddening circumstance of all for Laura was her sense of being constantly stymied, unable to improve the relationship (or uncertain she wanted to try anymore), and equally unable to leave. Her difficulty finding her inner compass, which could direct her towards a resolution, is probably the same dilemma you face if you see yourself and your partner manifesting these interlocking patterns.

Just as the narcissist has been reinforcing his loyalty to his own special needs, you have consciously or unconsciously been reinforcing your devotion to your partner's needs, at times to martyr-like extremes. In addition, you may have been developing tradeoffs or compromises that attempt to reconcile the emptiness you are tolerating. You have perhaps thrown yourself into your job, your children, improvements in your lifestyle with better things, schools for the kids, vacations, and so on.

Sometimes, you may have consciously decided to join him in the pursuit of money and status hoping that this will alleviate your suffering. Eventually, you may become as incapable as your NPD partner to recognize your own false self—the vital support person or the gracious hostess. Despite your potential denial, you will probably be the partner who recognizes that the relationship is in jeopardy for the simple reason that your defenses leave you more vulnerable to the experience of burn-out.

The defenses involved in codependency cause a process of self-reflection in one sense as you try to continually reassess what you might be doing to create such painful disruptions in the relationship, or how to satisfy or fix your partner. On the other hand, you will notice that this self-reflection tends to consist of ruminations about what your partner may think, often trying to figure out how he thinks and feels, rather than a reflection of your own beliefs and desires. The ongoing deprivation of *your* emotional needs will eventually wear you down, perhaps in the form of depression, stress-related symptoms, or addictions. As the partner working overtime in the relationship, you are the one experiencing more conscious pain, desperate to find emotional relief. Therefore, you will probably be the partner who begins to signal genuine warnings that your relationship is in danger.

A potentially rude awakening is to realize that the degree of unhealthy narcissism in your partner may signal the degree of unhealthy narcissism in yourself on the codependent side of the relationship. Unfortunately, if you can't take responsibility for your own defensive passivity, then your narcissistic partner will be unlikely to take responsibility for his defensive self-centeredness. Your interaction together becomes a perfect mutual dependence. Termed "symbiotic," this dependence is a continual reinforcement of each other's primary defense. By contrast, when you *do* take responsibility to deal with your passive dynamics and the wounds to your own sense of self, you are able to know and assert your true feelings in the relationship. Your increasing ability to stand up for yourself will simultaneously surface your partner's willingness and/or capacity to address his or her problems.

As Laura examined her feelings about her relationship, she marveled at the extent to which she tolerated her husband's disrespectful treatment and was exasperated by her tendency to feel responsible for this treatment. One day she came to therapy reporting a more extreme episode of verbal abuse on her husband's part. Following this behavior, she had asserted her desire for relationship therapy in a calm and caring way. He responded by venting outrage that she would bring the matter up again and threatened to end the marriage if she wasn't satisfied.

After Laura recounted her story, she expressed dismay that she was putting up with such humiliating treatment. Then, like the two sides of a Greek chorus, she went on to explain why she could not really hold her husband accountable for his misdeeds. She explained that in her heart she knew she did not love him and more often than not felt bitterness towards him. How could she expect him to be a loving partner when she felt no love towards him? Although the escalating pattern of abuse was as severe as before, her confusion was equally intense. She remained stuck and torn between her many conflicting feelings.

Laura's inability to change the direction of her life despite her increasing pain was due to the fact that she continued to perpetuate her own false self, a self that covers up and pretends, never expressing the true nature of her feelings. *No matter how extreme our pain might become, we cannot make a decision that emanates from the false self of codependency. The confidence we so desperately need comes only from our authentic self.* How could she confront her husband's narcissism when she could not acknowledge and legitimize her honest feelings? Laura's dead-end was the trap of her own false self, the grandiose care taker.

In the process of therapy Laura uncovered several false beliefs that she had internalized. She realized that she unconsciously believed that love is only defined by the willingness to sacrifice her own needs for the needs of others. Consequently, when she made efforts to assert her needs, she felt that she was betraying the relationship. When we put this equation in stark relief she could see the falseness of such a belief.

Love (only) = Sacrificing my needs for the needs of others therefore . . .
Asserting my needs as equal in my relationship = Betrayal

In short, her feelings of betrayal with her husband were a projection of her own self-betrayal—a betrayal that originated once upon a time in childhood so that she could feel loved. We can easily see how Laura's distortions about love and her own needs would make it impossible to take the necessary actions to confront her husband's narcissism and hold her ground (especially when we add the fear of her husband's impressive demonstrations of anger). Eventually, Laura's courageous forays beyond the familiar security of her defenses allowed her to claim her genuine feelings and express herself more honestly in the relationship.

Until we can acknowledge our feelings with honesty, we cannot assert with confidence our perception of what is false in another person, especially the false self of our partner. To end the continuous spiraling of each partner's false self in the relationship, there must be an interruption in the pattern. One or both partners must have the courage to expose the charade by claiming the right to a life of authenticity. Laura could only end her stalemate by taking a stand for her feelings, which in turn allowed her to discover what she really wanted regarding the relationship. In a parallel fashion to the discovery of her true self, she simultaneously was able to discern her partner's capacity and/or motivation for change. In Laura's case, she decided to end the relationship and was able to carry this out with a sense of peace and determination.

The discovery of your own truth offers the leverage and capability you have always had but didn't know—the power to resolve your struggle and find peace. As you consider asserting an ultimatum to your partner, you may anticipate his or her reaction and dread opening "Pandora's box." You intuitively know that she will recognize your determination and will place all her manipulative efforts in the direction of winning you over again. Perhaps she will do this with a show of repentance along with a convincing display of intentions to mend her ways. You may also fear her ability to turn things around, targeting you for the many misunderstandings in the relationship. Consequently, you may be profoundly conflicted with a mixed array of feelings as you offer her an ultimatum to go to therapy. As the codependent partner entering relationship therapy, you may feel:

- Enraged that you had to get to the point of leaving the relationship for her to listen and be willing to work on the relationship problems.

- Angry that he now shows such earnest desire and concern, undermining your confidence about reality.

- Guilt and self-doubt about the fairness of your own dealings with her since she is showing so much desire to change.
- Confused about what you want as you see him make such ardent efforts to woo you back. Relief that perhaps things really can change.
- Hope mixed with fear about the chances for genuine change.
- Anxiety that by giving him another chance you will destroy the last bit of independent self-assertion you have, meanwhile undermining your position when he no longer fears that you will leave.
- Fear that a therapist will join her in discrediting your feelings and needs that you have fought so hard to take a stand for.
- Enraged that you have to sort through your confused feelings all over again.

Perhaps this list includes only a few of the many emotions that you have when your narcissistic partner places himself at your feet to give him another chance. Even if you have no desire at this time to rebuild the relationship, you are unlikely to lose anything by asserting your thoughts and feelings in the relationship. You may need your own support person, preferably a therapist (someone other than your relationship therapist), so that you can continue to work on your codependency issues while you work on the possibilities for change with your partner. As you commit to this work, you will recognize the undeniable benefit of learning more about yourself and your partner regardless of the outcome.

Knowing you can't lose by addressing the relationship issues out in the open can help you to dive into the process even when you are still unsure of what you really want. When you choose a relationship therapist wisely, you can also be assured of the support and assistance of a neutral third party to ensure that communication is fair. Wherever you are on the continuum of hope, relationship therapy offers you an opportunity to strengthen and heal your authentic self and to achieve a greater resolution about your decisions, no matter what they are.

Sometimes you may have unique circumstances that are important to take into account, especially if there is a history of physical abuse or if you have reason to fear significant potential harm resulting from your ultimatum. In cases like these, you must have the support and advice of a therapist as you assert your efforts toward change. You may also need legal advice so that you can protect yourself from possible retaliation on your husband or wife's part to play hardball in a divorce action. In the scenario of disengaging from a relationship with an NPD partner, you will need to utilize a number of self-care strategies; here again the support and help of a therapist and friends will be vital.

A more encouraging scenario would involve your partner's cooperation to attend therapy before you have arrived at the end of the road. In this instance, you may still have desire and hope for an improved relationship. The journey of discovery and healing in couple's therapy can be a profoundly rewarding experience when both partners demonstrate a willingness and ability to work towards healing and growth. When this occurs, the possibilities for intimacy and fulfillment can be wonderfully surprising. Regardless of how confused or hopeful you are about your relationship, your decision to begin a proactive process of healing may be the most significant turning point of your adult life.

At this point, I should mention one exception to the pattern of the codependent partner as the initiator of therapy. Sometimes the NPD partner may be the one who insists on therapy if he has become dissatisfied or upset with your increasing demonstration of indifference, distance, or emotional decline. These scenarios will tend to involve the NPD partner's mission to fix you—his disturbed partner—as he confidently attends the therapy expecting to play co-therapist in the sessions. Despite his attitude, however, he can become enlightened regarding his own set of problems and defenses if he is motivated to work and does not have the full narcissistic personality disorder.

The most painful scenario occurs when the NPD partner who has been having an affair initiates therapy under the auspices of making the relationship better. Meanwhile, he is waiting to leave once he feels you are "stronger," have support, and can withstand the shock of learning that the marriage is over. You will notice that when the NPD partner does initiate the therapy, he rarely does so recognizing that he has any significant psychological problems of his own. Likewise, he will not expect to be delving into his own behaviors other than superficially.

Regardless of the circumstance that brings you both into therapy, you will need to research a qualified relationship therapist, preferably someone who specializes in couple's therapy and has a good reputation among his or her colleagues. You will want to find a relationship therapist who has skills in teaching more effective communication as well as training and talent in the important process of insight development. In other words, the therapist needs to be experienced in working with both partners *together* (not separately) as she helps them develop insight into their defenses, which are connected to themes of childhood wounding. Choosing an individual and/or relationship therapist will be discussed further in the appendix. At this point, I will simply recommend that you choose a relationship therapist that is fresh to both of you and not associated with one or the other through an individual therapy relationship.

As I begin to work with couples entrenched in these defensive patterns, I have been surprised and encouraged to discover that both partners are often willing to listen to an educational presentation on my part that outlines these very concepts. In fact, I have seen continued evidence that the narcissistic partner can be surprisingly open to this information. If the narcissistic partner is more within the continuum of narcissistic traits as opposed to the character disorder, he may find enormous relief to have the vicious cycle of his defenses given a name and an explanation that can help him begin the journey back to his authentic self. This level of work is, of course, only possible after a certain degree of trust has been established between the couple and therapist.

The first issue you must address within the relationship is leveling the playing field for fair communication. With issues of narcissism present in one or both of you, you undoubtedly have a painful history of escalated fighting that has contributed significantly to the deterioration in the relationship. Perhaps the destructive fighting between you *is* the main issue. If you cannot gain your partner's cooperation to attend therapy (which is generally your first choice) you can still obtain some valuable resources that will expose your partner to tools that inform and teach about the importance of following ground rules for fair fighting.

Many relationship therapy experts are using some form of structured dialogue that inserts ground rules into the process, most notably, Harville Hendrix, Ph.D.'s *imago* approach and the PREP- Program of therapy experts Blumberg, Markman, and Stanley, Ph.D.s. The latter group demonstrates research that indicates that *the number one predictor for the long-term success of any relationship is how well the couple is able to handle conflict.* Since most, if not all, couples need help in this area when they first enter therapy, this is usually the first order of business for relationship work. A book that focuses on this set of skills is *Difficult Conversations*, by Stone, Patton, and Heen.

Alongside the importance of elevating your ability to handle conflict together, you will generally find that you each gain a tool that increases your sense of safety and self-esteem. As the codependent partner, you achieve validation and assistance in confronting your partner's destructive aggressive behaviors, and your narcissistic partner appreciates these tools because they allow a clear structure that will ensure "fair play," a vital support to the brittle unconscious defenses of the NPD partner. Working with mutually agreed-upon ground rules also reframes the problem by externalizing it as *a problem you are working on together* rather than personalizing every issue due to the deadlock of your different positions. Finally, these tools allow you to demonstrate your commitment to resolve an issue, no matter how difficult, while relying on a structure that prevents the escalation of critical and blaming behaviors.

Although you should not expect to implement new ground rules for communication successfully on your own, you can gain an orientation to them. As you try to employ these strategies in your relationship, you will quickly recognize why you need a therapist who can help you learn to apply them. You may find it virtually impossible to incorporate new coping strategies during conflict (a time when defenses are at their peak) without a third person who can help each of you recognize and interrupt the powerful dynamic of your defensive pattern.

If you cannot gain the cooperation of your partner to work with you in raising the level of behavior when conflict arises, you can still enforce your own decision to maintain a higher standard. In this scenario I am assuming that you have been unable to enlist your partner's efforts to work on the relationship. Therefore, I would encourage you to obtain the support of a therapist in individual therapy who can help you sort through the confusing array of issues you face. Unilaterally raising the level of conflict by enforcing certain ground rules on your own will require the use of the "time out" intervention, a central rule used in relationship therapy.

"Time out" involves the practice of stopping yourself and/or your partner from indulging in the angry defensive sparring match that easily escalates into "dirty fighting." In addition to insisting on a "time out," you can state your intention to discuss the issue again when cooler heads can prevail. Regardless of your partner's cooperation within or outside the context of relationship therapy, *it is imperative that you begin to set limits on his verbal abuse or intimidation as well as to resist the impulse to explode into angry ventilation yourself. This may be the most difficult work you will do.*

If you do not have the support of couple's therapy to assist you in using this new tool, then you will need to let your partner know (at a calm and sober moment) that you will not continue to discuss an issue when it escalates into an argument. You can let him know that you will request a "time out" when things get heated and you both fall into the problematic interaction of escalated fighting. You need to inform him that you will adhere to this assertion by removing yourself from his presence if he doesn't honor your request. To ensure that your request for a time out is perceived as "fair play," you must also include your intention to continue the discussion as soon as possible when you have both calmed down, and when you can discuss the issue without criticism and personal attack.

A "time out" may also be necessary when you need time to think about criticisms he levels at you so that you can gather some perspective about your own thoughts. As mentioned in chapter three, your narcissistic partner may employ many subtle defensive behaviors that confuse and intimidate you. Allowing yourself time to consider how you really feel about something is a helpful intervention that will strengthen your ability to stand your ground.

The tendency for your NPD partner to refuse to talk with you about a sensitive issue is perhaps a more common dynamic in your communication stalemates. Your temptation to "trigger" her or "engage" her in discussions without her prior agreement will invariably play into the escalation of destructive conflict. Regardless of your inability to resolve problems together, your commitment and determination to prevent escalation and fighting will go a long way to encourage her to discuss matters with you at other times.

A central communication tool taught in couple's therapy is a process that is given many different names depending on your therapist's relationship therapy training. You may find it reassuring to know that most of the experts in the field of relationship work are using similar forms of the same tool. The variety of names given to this process are: "dialogue, mirroring, active listening, the speaker/listener technique, reflective listening," and so on. In general, this process includes an agreement that partners take turns talking and listening while including a discipline that requires the listener to reflect back, or "mirror," the message that the speaker is sending.

Although there are several variations of this tool, the essential idea is for partners to learn to listen and understand each other without the interference of their defenses. This process allows each partner to have an opportunity to be heard no matter how contrasting or different the opinions may be. Couples begin to recognize and respect that they are both entitled to their own legitimate feelings regardless of how they differ. As partners achieve greater safety and mutual respect for each other, they are now in *contact* with one another. While resolving a given issue may still be down the road, partners are now engaged in a true dialogue with the beginnings of genuine understanding, or the hope of achieving understanding.

Seemingly simple, this practice is far more challenging than most couples can handle on their own at first. The programming that we all have imbedded in our psyches is the false belief that to listen and reflect back what we hear our partner say will be heard as agreement. Our fear of losing our own reality to the reality of our partner is so strong that we have the automatic impulse to interrupt and try to override our partner's message with that of our own. You can see how much effort (and support) may be required to develop enough mutual trust that both of you are willing to honor such restrained and respectful communication.

For the moment, you must begin with the basic practice of learning to stop the escalation that usually results in destructive words in a matter of seconds. Recognizing and enforcing the "time out" tool will help empower you in two ways—increased self-care by preventing exposure to the devaluing behaviors, and heightened objectivity toward the relationship by limiting your own destructive input. Opting out of the temptation to have your own tantrum will remove the guilt you may feel over your behavior and allow you to maintain a more objective perspective on the issue.

You may be thinking I "must be kidding," because it is never possible to discuss any difficult issue calmly. Whenever you do get his attention, he perhaps demonstrates a complete intolerance to hear you before he immediately launches into his formidable defenses of cool critical analysis or an angry outburst that is often frightening. Regardless of this pattern, however, you are beginning to assert your right to respectful consideration and a fair expression of your thoughts and feelings in the relationship. You must begin by challenging his "Oz-like" intimidation defenses and refuse to take the bait of his forceful ability to draw you into the ring for a fight. He is well aware (whether consciously or unconsciously) that he is ten times the fighter that you are. He may even take considerable pleasure in venting his pent-up emotional steam. Meanwhile, he may also disown any responsibility in the whole affair later since, after all, YOU were the one who "started it."

You will remember from chapter three that the other fundamental skill you need to develop is an awareness of healthy versus unhealthy boundaries. Your NPD partner's tendency to create boundary confusion and boundary intrusion is the central and most destructive dynamic at play. The NPD individual's ability to sound convincing, as though he has the objective truth, is a potent force that often causes you to abdicate your feelings and needs, giving up the boundaries that define you.

Frequently, the NPD person labels his partner's feelings as "hysterical," a buzzword used to diminish the validity of his partner's perspective. This criticism is generally a projection of the NPD partner's denial of his emotions and the belief that feelings are irrational and therefore illegitimate. You may remember from chapter three that the defenses common to the NPD are: repetitive criticism (and other devaluing behaviors), aggressive intimidation (countered by your abdication), distraction through defocusing the issues, projection, and double-message/double-bind tendencies.

Boning up on your ability to recognize the defenses so commonly seen in unhealthy narcissism will help you to assert your need for a time out to reflect and determine what's going on. As we discussed in chapters three through five, the more difficult defenses to recognize and to address will be those of projection and the double-message because they are much more embedded in the unconscious themes connected to childhood wounding. However, once you can identify and surface these dynamics, you will feel significantly more in control of your reactions with a greater ability to confront the behaviors that are out of bounds.

If your partner never attends therapy with you, your evaluation and work on the relationship will involve your efforts towards self-care through individual growth and healing and your attempts to raise the level of interaction on your own. Regular reminders to your partner that you are changing and that you expect him to take his share of responsibility for the relationship problems are essential steps towards getting out of the quagmire of your stalemate. Meanwhile you are gaining a new sense of yourself and what your priorities are. Ultimately you will be making important decisions about what you expect from your relationship and whether or not you are willing to settle for less.

As we have discussed throughout this book, the issues connected to narcissistic wounding are generally unconscious since they have their origins in an early pattern of childhood wounding. One remarkable advantage to couple's therapy is that the struggles between you and your partner point the way like an arrow to the otherwise cryptic and forgotten history of your childhood. Developing insight into your own childhood wounding can be much easier to accomplish in the forum of couple's therapy.

Harville Hendrix's imago therapy approach begins the relationship work by teaching a similar set of communication skills with a few helpful additions. In my experience, imago therapy is one of the few models of relationship therapy that includes a set of tools to help partners understand the connection of their relationship "issues" to the unconscious or conscious childhood wounding experiences. In other words, the struggles and painful battles that go on in a relationship are inevitably a re-enactment of the painful struggles each partner experienced in childhood. Because the power struggle is deeply rooted in unconscious forces connected to childhood wounding, both partners unwittingly participate in the increasing misunderstanding and misjudgment of one another. Eventually, the conflict and misunderstanding can damage the empathy and love between partners beyond repair.

In a nutshell, whether you utilize imago therapy or another form of relationship therapy, *you will need to find a therapy that places the development of empathy at the very center of the relationship work.* All the skills that you will learn must be aimed at restoring and developing your own and your partner's ability for mutual respect and empathy. Empathy (which is the ability to emotionally understand and or connect with another person) is *the* ability that is lacking for the narcissistic individual. Because the only way to truly change and heal this problem is to rediscover and claim the cut-off feelings from childhood, all other avenues of attempting to restore empathy will generally be superficial. Just offering a set of instructions to the partner on how to behave empathically would not only be a temporary fix, but potentially another re-enactment of childhood wounding because a partner may feel that he or she is only pretending all over again.

The development of empathy is the core issue in your relationship with your narcissistic partner because it is empathy that has been sacrificed in the adoption of the "false self." Therapy must assist in the development of empathy both in the here and now through the use of effective communication tools and in the development of insight and emotional healing work regarding each partner's childhood histories. Good relationship therapy needs to be a combination of learning new communication skills as well as developing an atmosphere of trust and readiness to conduct the deeper levels of emotional healing. To understand the approach to healing work in imago therapy, I recommend Harville Hendrix's enlightening book, *Getting the Love You Want: A Guide for Couples.*

The relevance of each partner's childhood history and unresolved emotional issues cannot be sidestepped, no matter how much we would wish to do so. As we discussed in chapter five, powerful forces are at play, forces that reinforce our many rationalizations to not explore, not know, and not feel the emotional pain of our early lives. And perhaps the most discouraging understanding in all of this is that the more intensely a person has been narcissistically wounded in childhood, the more intensely he or she will manifest a defense of denial and repression of this wounding. Consequently, you will need to find an experienced therapist who can increase the chances of engaging the narcissistic partner at this level. The encouraging news is that your partner may be more likely to allow this work to take place in couple's therapy because he won't be alone, and he will feel less "on the spot" with both of you exploring your deeper "issues" together.

One of the hallmarks indicating the degree of unhealthy narcissism that I have witnessed again and again is a pronounced and almost unreal depiction on the part of the narcissistic partner of a "normal" and wholesome childhood, a childhood filled with the devoted efforts of parents to raise "good" children. While the codependent partner is generally more in touch with the difficulties of her childhood, the NPD partner will describe his early life like the Ozzie and Harriett TV show (often citing this show as a reference). The powerful nature of the defenses of denial and idealization are a source of wonder indeed when this individual uncovers a history of significant (at times traumatic) narcissistic wounding to his or her sense of self.

Equally remarkable to your partner's defenses can be your own defenses in the form of self-abdication through a focus on care-taking others. Your denial may be the belief that you have arrived on the other side of the healing process. You therefore believe that your efforts are put to better use in supporting your partner in addressing his "unfinished business" from childhood. Your discomfort with feelings of anger, especially in your relationship, are often as difficult and illusive to recognize as your NPD partner's feelings of vulnerability are for him.

As you develop greater ability and strength to live from your authentic self, eventually you will determine your partner's capacity for becoming more authentic with herself and with you. If your partner continues to show a significant pattern of denial and backsliding into her narcissistic defenses despite the relationship therapy, contrasted by your increased ability to be authentic in the relationship, you may have surfaced the difference in capacity between you and your partner for true intimacy. On the other hand, if your partner demonstrates a slow but progressive ability to recognize her defenses and shows continued improvement and desire to grow, you may be feeling significant relief with the improved quality of your emotional connection. As these insights unfold, you will be exploring the soul-searching questions about what you want out of life and your relationship. You will discover more clearly what you are willing to fight for in order to feel an inner peace and contentment about your choices.

In the end, you will be making a choice from one of the three potential possibilities:

1. End the relationship. You recognize that your NPD partner's limitations for love and intimacy are too severe. To stay in the relationship requires the profound sacrifice of your needs and your sense of *self* and continually leaves you with deep feelings of loss and loneliness. In this scenario, you decide to leave the relationship.

2. Maintain the relationship with a commitment to self-care. You decide that the losses involved in leaving the relationship are too great. In this alternative, you realize that your partner's limitations will require your constant maintenance to meet your baseline needs; however, the losses involved in leaving are greater. Perhaps in this alternative, you have spent a lifetime invested in this relationship and/or you have children that you are unwilling to share part-time. Whatever the reasons, you feel that staying together will provide you with sufficient fulfillment.

3. Transform the relationship. Of course, this is the outcome you would hope for and one that is indeed possible if both partners are capable of and motivated for true self-reflection and change. In this scenario, both of you are committed to the hard work of compassionate honesty, a soul-searching effort to forgive, and an ongoing recognition that intimacy is a "work in progress" and a lifelong commitment.

Forgiveness

Forgiveness is the last leg of your journey before you can experience a completely different kind of love than you have known in your relationship before. As you grapple with your partner to heal the many wounds of the past, you will ultimately grapple with the deeper and more potent issues of forgiveness.

The narcissistic partner, while having made remarkable and undeniable change, will often feel a resentment and impatience that you are too slow in your ability to let go of the past and truly forgive him. He may (with some justification) feel stymied as he begins to feel that you will never accept him for who he is, despite his genuine efforts to change. He has difficulty understanding that you need many opportunities to discuss the hurt you experienced for all the times you felt abandoned and betrayed by him. His lesson is patience and empathy and the ability to see his narcissistic behaviors in a more objective light.

Misunderstanding the notion of forgiveness can stall you in your efforts to forgive your partner, which is in truth, the unfinished business of your own narcissistic wounding. As the codependent, you may become frustrated with yourself as you realize that forgiveness is not a matter of intellectual desire or even the natural result of your partner's sincere and significant changes. It is important to realize that forgiveness does not imply that you must stop expressing your feelings of dissatisfaction, hurt, and anger about the past and similar infractions in the present. Nor does it mean that your partner is not accountable for his continued efforts towards change.

Forgiveness is the ability to have enough empathy and understanding to feel genuine compassion towards your partner and an abiding compassion for yourself—a forgiveness that realizes that his betrayal and your own self-betrayal are the result of your histories of wounding and unwitting participation to perpetuate it. This compassion must be developed through the deeper understanding of your own and your partner's journey through life. Each partner must forgive the false self of the other and recognize the childhood wounding that required the development of such a false self. Indeed, you will need to evidence your partner's continued commitment to cast off the defensive layers just as you must continue to let go of your own. Ultimately, your inability to forgive in your heart rests on the existence of unresolved grief surrounding a deeper wounding experience, one that predates your relationship with your partner—your original experience of betrayal and narcissistic wounding in childhood.

Because the narcissist and the codependent are essentially manifest-ing opposite faces of wounding to the self, both are challenged to recognize their unhealthy narcissism and come to terms with it. My favorite analogy to these two faces exists in the wonderful story that Jesus taught in the parable of the prodigal son, a discussion of which is included at the end of this chapter. It is undoubtedly no accident that a story revealing the different pictures of narcissism is also one about for-giveness.

As you commit to the journey of self-discovery and claim your birth-right to experience and express your feelings, you will be liberated from the oppression of your defenses and false self. This liberation (when genuine) will release you from feelings of bitterness about the past be-cause you can truly mourn the losses and empathize with the legacy of "unfinished business" that has been handed down from one generation to the next. You will feel the confidence that comes with the certainty of knowing your feelings.

The ability to recognize your own unhealthy narcissism will em-power you to speak out against the unhealthy narcissism in your partner. Your choices involving your relationship will also become clear to you as you claim a life of authenticity. When you can build your relation-ship on the sacred ground of truth and love, you will find the fulfillment and contentment of true intimacy—an intimacy of love that comes from the deep knowing of another person and, in turn, of being known.

The Prodigal Son and the Older Brother— Forgiveness and the Two Faces of Narcissism

The story of the prodigal son is probably the most widely known parable from the *New Testament* of the *Holy Bible* (Luke 15:12) and undoubtedly one of the most powerful stories Jesus used to teach les-sons of forgiveness.

In the prodigal son parable, we can look through two lenses to see the issues of unhealthy narcissism and the "false self." The more obvi-ous depiction of destructive narcissism is, of course, seen in the prodigal son, whose entitlement and self-indulgence are evidenced by his re-quest for his inheritance early (while his father is living) and his subsequent dismissal of all responsibility as he squanders this inheritance. Eventually, he descends into total depravation and demonstrates a defiant disregard for anything but his own pleasure. After a lengthy time of self-indulgence, the self-made trap of his isolated squalor teaches him the lessons of his grandiosity.

Finally, the prodigal son is able to embrace the truth about himself and come to terms with his "ordinariness." He is neither completely depraved nor above the struggle to work for his living. Seeking a new life, he returns to his father's house and hopes to be taken in as a servant to live out his days as a common man in his father's house. His contrition and his expectation reveal his true attitude. He does not expect forgiveness from his father, but by working in his father's house, he hopes to salvage his life from further descent. This last insight reflects his acceptance of his full self (his past and his future) without resentment or self-pity. Similarly, he is able to accept his father's forgiveness with gratitude and joy, demonstrating an ability to forgive himself. This same patient and accepting attitude will be the goal of the narcissistic partner as he realizes who he has been and who he truly is.

At this point in the story, we learn about the feelings and attitude of the eldest brother who has led a "righteous" life, working hard to fulfill the expectations and responsibilities that were given to him. He resents his father's forgiveness of the prodigal brother and feels outrage that his brother should be restored to full status. His feelings begin to unveil the hidden narcissism of his own false self as we see his unforgiving attitude. The moment of reunion reveals the lack of love that resides behind the narcissism of "cleaving to good" as a false or substitute self. The subtle narcissism of the older brother is perhaps more difficult to expose since this brother has devoted his entire life to doing "the right thing," living the life of an obedient, hard-working, and respectful son. We must see his inability to love before we can detect any falseness in such a person of goodness.

The two forms of narcissism exposed in the prodigal son story beg provocative questions. In which form of self-deception may we be more likely to discover our dishonesty and, therefore, reclaim our true selves? The self-indulgent "rebel" or "con artist" is perhaps less likely to delude himself about his behavior. He knows his actions are illegitimate! However, his lack of conscience or empathy for the destructive impact he has on others will prevent him from seeing the truth. He will have to endure the painful consequences of his conduct before he can see the grandiosity that is so out of control.

On the other hand, the self-righteous narcissism portrayed in a life of impeccable goodness also prevents the recognition of falseness since this person fully believes that his life reflects nothing but goodness and grace. His false pride must be exposed by his "empathic failures"—his inability to forgive and accept the full humanity in others and ultimately in himself. After all, how can we say that goodness is good without love? Only when the older brother is challenged to forgive and love his brother with all his faults and failures do we see the narcissism of the eldest brother. In fact, what other means would allow the discovery of unhealthy narcissism in a person who has demonstrated a life of correct living since we cannot see his attitude towards his own human failings?

Our inability to forgive is based on our inability to grieve the loss and disconnection we have experienced with our true and whole self, a self with strengths and failings, a self with the full range of positive and negative emotions. The prodigal son must discover the choices that perpetuated a life of defiant self-indulgence. The righteous brother must realize his falseness when he encounters his resentment and inability to forgive. Yet, his unwillingness to forgive by itself may not help him recognize his own unhealthy narcissism. He, too, will require consequences before he can see the grandiosity of his false pride.

The final scene in this story is the father's gentle admonishment to his eldest son for his lack of spiritual generosity. Perhaps this consequence creates the pain necessary for him to realize his narcissism. We do not know the end of the story concerning the elder brother because we are not told if he follows his father and younger brother into the house to participate in the celebration. Perhaps he must struggle with the pain of his first conscious separation between his father and himself. This conscious awareness may help him to recognize his feelings surrounding a deeper loss and to develop a genuine empathy as he recognizes his own capacity for narcissism. The humility gained in the retrieval of his authentic self will become the counterpart to his prodigal brother's transformation, and both men may then celebrate in the joy of their healing.

CHAPTER SIX SUMMARY

The initial phase of the love relationship is often characterized by intense feelings of intoxication and an ardent pursuit on the part of the narcissist. Only after you fully invest yourself emotionally do you enter the inner sanctum of your NPD partner and discover the dark side of his false self. At this point, the NPD partner's difficulty with intimacy is revealed by an increasing show of contempt for your "neediness." He may begin a pattern of criticism and temper outbursts, or cold withdrawal and detached indifference to your feelings.

The complementary defenses of codependence and narcissism are now fully engaged as you each continue to polarize the other. As the codependent, your need to be needed and accepted has potentially been growing into the role of "larger than life care taker of others" with your NPD partner. The NPD partner, with his unconscious feelings of inadequacy and fear of humiliation, is able to fully take the reigns in the relationship, increasing his entitlement demands for his "larger than life persona," whatever the role.

For you as the codependent, you cannot recognize your equal right to be loved, cared for, and supported in the relationship. You increasingly repress your anger and unconsciously manifest some form of the belief that to love means sacrificing your needs for the needs of your partner (to the exclusion of your own). In turn, your narcissistic partner becomes emboldened to demand more and give less, demonstrating an impressive ability to ignore your distress in the relationship. His "empathic failure" (inability to recognize your need for support and empathy) in the face of some critical event is commonly the trigger that causes you to recognize the falseness of your relationship and your need to seek help.

Healing and empowerment work must include a *continual balance* of effort in the form of *self-care and boundary setting*.

Self-Care
- Gain insight into your own codependent defenses.
- Develop the ability to validate your own thoughts and feelings.
- Recognize and legitimize your emotional needs.

- Identify your partner's narcissistic defenses and behaviors.
- Develop friendships and supportive relationships that nurture you.
- Heal and grieve deeper issues of childhood wounding.

Boundary Setting
- Practice assertiveness skills—especially within the relationship.
- Set limits on the unhealthy narcissistic demands of your partner and *stop* your exposure to your partner's emotionally abusive behaviors.
- Institute "fair fighting" ground rules—if necessary, unilaterally.
- Assert your thoughts and feelings with increasing regularity, using empowerment strategies of "dialogue" or "mirroring" communication.
- Communicate "warnings" about your distress with the problems in the relationship alongside the fact that your partner is equally responsible for working them out.
- Confront and "name" some of the defensive behaviors that you see in your partner and demonstrate a willingness to acknowledge your own.

Initially, these steps are difficult to keep in mind because, as the codependent partner, you will have a tendency to take in your new awareness through the lens of your defenses. Your tendency may be to learn new information about your NPD partner and feel that you must now enact the plan that will enable you to fix *him*. Your own narcissism, which stems from the care-taking side of the coin, prevents you from recognizing the depth and degree of work you must do with yourself.

When you feel strong enough to insist that your partner attend relationship therapy, you will need a therapist who can be neutral to both of you (someone who has not seen either partner individually). The type of relationship therapy that you choose must be one that puts the development of empathy at the center of the work. All of these efforts will create a healing of self-esteem, the recognition as to whether or not your partner is able to achieve more meaningful change, and the ability to determine the decision that is right for you regarding your relationship.

Are You a Good Witch or a Bad Witch?

The Social or Professional Relationship

The Friendship Relationship

When I get lost or end up somewhere I don't want to be, if I am honest with myself, I have to admit that I wasn't very clear about where I was going in the first place. When it comes to establishing friendships most of us follow that "feel good" sensation of the moment. After all, the idea of friendship can mean any number of things depending on the day, our mood, or the type of shared experience we are looking for. Friendship also means different things to different people. As a result, we enter into friendship relationships without asking ourselves many questions about what we are looking for and how much we are willing to invest. Even less, do we ask ourselves, what is the other person looking for? Is he or she on the same wavelength?

Friendships can have many levels, and we would be ahead of the game if we thought in terms of a kind of ranking. In other words, we might distinguish between those individuals who represent our closest friends and confidants, and those with whom we enjoy lesser degrees of closeness. We will have fewer disappointments if we are clear about what we expect from our various friendships, all the way down to those we simply enjoy on a more superficial or social level.

If these distinctions seem to require too much work, think back on a friendship that developed into drudgery, or perhaps a friendship that left you feeling burned or betrayed. Backpedaling out of a friendship

141

you don't really want, or the pain of recovering from a friendship that left you hurt, takes much more effort than the initial work of assessing what your potential new friend is made of in the first place.

When we discover that a friendship has become a one-way street, the unfortunate truth is that we probably weren't looking very carefully when we were in the acquaintance stage. On the other hand, in fairness to ourselves, we probably weren't aware of *what* to be looking for, or what to be looking *out* for! Stranded on the roadside, we end up feeling like a fool, a victim, or both.

Recently, as I was having a discussion with a seventeen-year-old young woman named Kalie, I realized that she was struggling to balance the give and take that is so illusive when dealing with an NPD individual. She had been having a lot of difficulty in her best friend relationship wondering what she was doing wrong, in short, whether or not her expectations and requests in the relationship were normal. Kalie was also beginning to recognize her tendency to seek approval and friendship by taking care of her friends and their needs, often at her own expense.

On this occasion Kalie was venting her anger and hurt that her friend could so easily write her off when she attempted to reassert an agreement they had made. She had been driving her friend Dana to and from school, as well as other places. In exchange, Dana had agreed that she would help Kalie with gas money. Over time, Dana began to neglect her part in the arrangement and when Kalie reminded her of her obligation, she responded with an indignant and reluctant attitude. Finally, one day when Kalie was trying to stretch the remainder of her weekly paycheck (about three dollars), she was literally driving on empty. When her friend called to ask her for a ride, Kalie had asserted that she simply couldn't drive her unless Dana could contribute for gas. This prompted a reaction of outrage from Dana who then hung up. Later when Kalie tried to initiate a discussion with Dana to talk it out, Dana was equally unwilling to meet her half way, refusing to talk about it. Kalie was now getting the big chill. In therapy, she discussed her disappointment that Dana's behavior was inherently unfair and made worse by her friend's unwillingness to discuss the matter.

Kalie was beginning to look at her pattern of friendship relationships. She started recognizing that she attracted friends who seemed unwilling or unable to give as well as take. Too often, she would only think to ask, "What am I doing wrong?" and rarely question her friend's capacities in the equation. Kalie's struggle with her friend Dana demonstrates the importance of reciprocal exchange. However, a more important lesson than this is at stake—the discovery of her friend's refusal to talk through their differences. If Kalie had not been able to assert her needs about their initial agreement (gas money for rides), she would not have discovered her friend's refusal to talk through a problem. She might have gone much further down the road giving and giving, only to feel more used and abused when she eventually made this discovery.

We also see the narcissistic/codependent dance in this vignette. After several months of cold, distancing behaviors, Dana demonstrated her desire to warm up to Kalie again. At this point, Kalie was aware that the unspoken understanding for friendship rested on the condition that she not discuss the problem that had caused their separation in the first place. *The tendency to ignore any need for deeper resolution is all too typical of the NPD individual who will want to wait it out until the conflict blows over.* Once the relationship resumes, the narcissistic individual will continue the defensive behaviors that influence the other person to conform to her rules of inter-relating. As Kalie tried to correct the imbalance of give and take regarding rides and gas money, she was met by the intimidation and devaluing defenses of her friend. With her friend's reluctance to talk through the problem, Kalie was confronted with the ultimate challenge to her codependency. Dana, in essence, was saying—you operate on my terms or no terms at all. Fortunately Kalie had developed a stronger sense of who she was and what she wanted. She was able to recognize that her friendship with Dana demanded more than she was willing to offer.

Kalie also began to identify her unconscious automatic behaviors that led to care taking as a way of gaining the acceptance and approval of her friends. She recognized that when she skipped the stage of evaluating a friend's capacity for *mutual* regard and effort she would inevitably become let down and possibly burned in the relationship. Kalie was learning to treat herself as a worthy person from the very beginning of her relationships, a skill that can be difficult if a person's survival role (since childhood) has been to gain love and acceptance through the care taking of others.

Like Kalie, if you are willing to self-reflect, you may notice that in addition to intimate relationships, the types of friendships you have also mirror back important lessons about yourself. If you are involved in friendships where you invariably end up giving more than receiving (as we have discussed in previous chapters) you are most likely suffering from codependency issues. You may have *over-learned* the skills of accommodating others: listening, supporting, and helping as part of your role growing up. As a result you may fall back on these qualities when you are establishing new relationships. Your care-taking tendencies can leave you blind to the important clues that will help you discover if a new friend is willing and able to participate in the reciprocal exchanges of energy, time, and resources that are a part of any blossoming friendship.

Overall, the ability to consider others and be concerned about their needs is a quality that is quite wonderful to have. However, when we always push the same character quality to the front of the line, *the virtues of listening, empathizing, and supporting quickly turn into the character defect of care-taking behaviors.* In the end, care taking is not only unhealthy for you, but for the other person too. For instance, Kalie's friend Dana didn't need another friend to gratify her narcissistic needs; she needed a friend who would confront her behaviors, offering her a chance to look at herself and grow.

If your role in childhood caused you to be over-identified with the characteristics of giving and self-sacrificing, this means that at a deep level you had normal narcissistic needs that were not met, and those needs that *were* met occurred more often as a result of your care-taking behaviors. Consequently, this sets up an unconscious tendency to be over-focused on "needing to be needed." The hidden side of this problem are issues with low self-esteem that make it difficult for you to feel equally deserving in the natural exchanges of support, attention, and priority regarding your needs.

As you explore your relationships with individuals that seem to repeatedly take more than they give, you will inevitably struggle with your self-doubt as you try to determine what to do about it. Similar to the relationships described in chapters four through six, you will encounter the struggle to validate your own perceptions of reality. While you may require a coach, therapist, or support person to assist you, you will eventually need to change your behaviors by asserting your feelings and needs in the relationship. As you take these courageous risks, you will discover your strengths and the capacity of your friend(s) to make equal efforts towards the give and take.

Your ability to achieve more mutually satisfying friendships will require a capacity to recognize your strengths and feel comfortable using them. Let's look at the continuum again from the standpoint of achieving a sense of healthy self. The more narcissistic, self-absorbed, or "me focused" an individual is, the more she is caught in the perpetual striving to feel important, valued, stable, and secure. The codependent individual, who is "other focused," is stuck striving for a sense of self by gaining and maintaining the acceptance and approval of others (primarily through their ability to give—especially empathy). *The narcissistic individual typically externalizes her flaws onto others* and defends against the self-reflection that would require developing empathy for others. Similarly, *the codependent is the person who internalizes the flaws of others onto herself* and defends against recognizing her need to develop her strengths through self-assertion and self-care.

Since we primarily understand things through comparison and contrast, we need to recognize both sides of the coin with regard to healthy and unhealthy narcissism and, likewise, healthy from unhealthy caring. When we can recognize the relative balance of this continuum, we can then act in ways that will help us establish and maintain satisfying friendships. Finally, we will feel more fulfillment in our friendships when we are honest with ourselves about our expectations, allowing for a "ranking of friendships"- those friends we are willing to invest our time and efforts in and those who remain primarily social relationships.

The Narcissist in the Workplace

Since our whole culture is based on the capitalistic principle of competition, the workplace is the arena where "getting ahead" is first and foremost. Fewer corporations and businesses bother themselves with the ethics of fair play or concern themselves with the fact that employees are human beings trying to live a quality life. In such an atmosphere of toughness, where "all's fair," you will see the NPD individual flourish and rise to the top.

So you must be on your guard, because no one can play tougher, meaner, and more cleverly than the NPD individual. We certainly see enough movies that portray how narcissism is rewarded in business—*Wall Street, Glengarry Glen Ross, Working Girl,* and the all time classic, *Citizen Kane* are but a few examples. *Unhealthy narcissism is primarily, first and last, competitive.* You will recall the dangerous manipulations that we discussed in chapter three regarding the dynamics of power. The end result of toxic narcissism is the imperative to be one up, with the other person one down, or to have more of something than the next person. In the workplace this boils down to money, power, and status!

The NPD businessperson is acutely aware of who is getting what in terms of recognition, opportunity, and power-making decisions. The ability to gain influence over potential competitors is a drive that will not abate until the NPD individual has surpassed that person or neutralized any threat to his own goal. Consequently, you must achieve a bottom line of boundary setting ability with this person. This is essential if you are going to prevent problems or defend yourself effectively from the NPD coworker or, worse yet, the NPD boss. Along with protecting yourself from hurt, exploitation, or betrayal, we are also now talking about self-preservation in terms of your career.

As we discussed in chapter three, you may not be immediately aware of the presence of this disorder in a person until she feels displeased with you in some way. Initially, in fact, if you have something that an NPD colleague wants, such as status, money, power, beauty, etc., she may pursue and shower you with attention in an effort to gratify you. However, as soon you become more closely involved with her, you will begin to feel the current of the one-way street. At first you may simply feel a sense of frustration that this person tends to distract you from your work, perhaps requiring an excess of attention and support. Inevitably, over time, you will have stronger feelings of frustration and exasperation, as well as a growing uneasiness about the relationship. Let's again look at questions you might ask yourself to determine the intensity of the narcissistic dynamic that may be present.

1. Do you get emotionally drained, preoccupied, or upset after your contacts with this person?
2. Do you begin to doubt yourself, your competence on the job, and feel insecure about his or her true opinion of you?
3. Are work performance expectations unclear and often changing?
4. Do you frequently feel frustrated, angry, or resentful after interactions with him or her?
5. Are you taking care of your own needs less and less?
6. Are you increasingly experiencing a confused mixture of feelings such as anxiety, intimidation, powerlessness, or inadequacy?

If these feelings are occurring with some regularity surrounding your interactions with this coworker or boss, you are possibly recognizing the NPD dynamic in him and witnessing any number of behaviors. For instance:

- You are receiving only a fraction of the support you give or recognition you deserve for your contributions.
- You are given conflicting or double messages regarding your responsibilities and performance.
- Your advancement may have been thwarted by an unfair review, or an endless delay of any review at all, giving you the message that you are unimportant.
- You have a sense that your credibility and competence in the eyes of others is being undermined.
- You may be feeling set up as "scapegoat," a frequent result of these relationships.

If these scenarios are beginning to unfold, then it is time for serious initiation of boundary setting and accountability strategies. In severe circumstances, you may need to end the relationship, if it is possible. However, if we are talking about an employer or coworker, you may have no choice about remaining in a working relationship with him. In this circumstance, it is time for nothing less than learning the basics of survival.

While you may want to try to work things through with the NPD colleague, keep in mind that, like Kalie and her friend Dana, constructive feedback will often be met with a defensive reaction and a serious distortion of your intention. Remember, if your business colleague does have the full narcissistic disorder, he is unlikely to change. Likewise, if you continue to placate him, you will only fall prey to more demands, and, in the end, unfair treatment.

Begin to set limits on the amount of time you are willing to listen to your NPD colleague and become more sparing in your praise and support. Identify and rehearse phrases that offer you a graceful exit from conversations or meetings. Pressing deadlines, important phone calls, even a restroom necessity can be assertive strategies to help you to limit your exposure to the NPD individual.

As you withdraw from some of your care-taking behaviors, be ready for the "change back" dynamics that we discussed in chapter five. You need to anticipate the NPD person's defensive response to feeling disappointed and deprived. Rehearse the assertiveness skill of calm resistance to avoid being drawn into combative interactions if the NPD colleague begins to assign blame or engages in faultfinding behaviors. Keep in mind the "one-way street" relationship to counteract any tendency towards guilt on your part. *Your unfounded guilt can be your worst enemy, causing you to try one more time to make him happy.*

Finally, use the leverage of your own expertise or productivity to keep the NPD person's behaviors in check. Be cautious as you offer your advice, remaining vigilant about what the NPD individual wants from you. Remember that any honeymoon period of cooperation you have with this person will last only as long as you have something she wants from you. Steel yourself for the moment when she projects her difficulties onto you. Be ready to stand up for yourself calmly and firmly without the expectation that she will acknowledge your position. For emotional support, utilize an outside support person (preferably out-

side the work setting, or an ironclad safe person within the work setting) who can validate your efforts and encourage you to stand up for
yourself.

If you are a person who hates paperwork (as I do), you are not going
to like what I have to say here. Your number one ally in the workplace is
to keep a daily log of your work efforts, even if it is only general—
perhaps merely a sentence or two describing your actions in the morning
and afternoon. (You will also notice that increasing your accountability
system tends to improve your own overall performance. This in turn
increases your self-confidence.) Document any task of significance with
specific descriptions of your progress alongside notations of relevant
discussions you had about the project. This daily journal should be private—for your records only, allowing you to have a factual source of
information in the event that more formal documentation may be
needed: for instance, your yearly review. This personal log will help you
validate your own reality if the NPD individual attempts to undermine
what you believe took place.

Memos highlighting new decisions are also safety mechanisms, as
well as memos summarizing discussions you had with your boss on
matters relevant to your performance. These are public records, and
you will want to send a copy to all individuals concerned. Two things
are automatically taken care of here:

1. You clear up any misunderstandings that may have occurred by
    creating an accountability system for communication.

2. You will surface and/or mitigate any resistance on your boss's part
    to clearly state his or her expectations of you. You may remember
    that the NPD individual is often engaged in sending double mes-
    sages that keep you off balance such as changing the rules in
    midstream while acting as if you had already been informed. The
    memo system is a good habit to get into for the sake of surfacing
    this problem *before* rather than *after* your job is in jeopardy.

I don't want to mislead you here. If you have an NPD employer
who is threatened by you and/or is making your life miserable, you may
only be, at best, in a position to implement damage control. You may
not be able to prevent the inevitable conclusion that you must find

another position or another job altogether. However, you will feel much better about yourself afterwards if you exercise more control over what unfolds.

Finally, you may need to enlist the involvement of a third person (whom you trust) during discussions of importance. The nastier things are getting, the more important this element will be. It may even reach the point where you *only* allow communication to occur when a third person is present. Utilizing the accountability systems available in the corporate setting, such as a grievance board, may also be useful. However, I probably don't need to spell out the fact that this is a strategy of last resort, since the NPD person will most likely wage all out war. In choosing a forum to air your grievances, you will need to be ready to make your case to a third party who may or may not be aware of, or sympathetic to, the deeper realities of dealing with a personality disordered individual.

Ultimately, you may be forced to make difficult choices about your career path in your present setting. When you can anticipate this decision in time to interview and obtain other employment, you are indeed acting from a place of strength. On the other hand, sometimes this is not possible, and you may need to cut your losses and simply bail out. Preserving your self-esteem with a proactive stance will be of utmost importance to you as you face your future. Sometimes protecting your self-esteem comes down to leaving the NPD employer or supervisor before he has the satisfaction of making you a scapegoat by demoting or firing you. In taking the initiative to leave, you are afforded the opportunity to reject the unfair, or even unethical, treatment you have experienced. Standing up for yourself will offer immeasurable solace to you as you face the challenge of restoring your self-esteem in the aftermath of your embroilment with the narcissist.

The cost of being degraded and dehumanized in a job generally far outweighs the cost of perceived risk in a period of unemployment. Having said this, however, every person's journey is unique in terms of circumstances and personal choices. Regardless of your choice, you must seek support people and develop potent coping skills through proactive efforts.

If these scenarios sound grim, I'm afraid it is because sometimes they are! Anyone who has walked the gauntlet of dealing with an NPD individual in the workplace knows full well how painful things can become. Your best protection is identifying this individual early in the game and employing self-preservation strategies.

The NPD Service Professional

Have you ever invested time and energy in acquiring a service from someone, and halfway into the project or process you wished you had never met this person? You discover that he isn't really interested in satisfying your needs as a consumer, but intends to do the job his way while meeting his needs first with a "too bad if you don't like it" attitude. By this time, your investment may be considerable, and it may be too costly to dismiss his services, a fact the NPD service professional well knows!

There is only one way I can recommend for warding off these disastrous business relationships—the interview technique. No matter what service you are seeking, allow yourself to thoroughly interview the person whose service you need. Let the person know that you are checking out your options and interviewing other individuals who offer the same service. Most importantly, take your time.

The healthier the person, the less likely he or she is to become defensive and impatient with you as you ask questions. On the one hand, the NPD individual, with his exquisite sensitivity to having his expertise questioned or to being compared to other individuals, may not be able to conceal his deeper feelings of anger. On the other hand, the camouflage of charm and confidence may be dazzling, and your investigation may require asking for the names of former customers or asking other experts in the field.

You will want to do a little research so that you can ask the questions that are important. Any service professional should be willing and able to tell you how they will approach your problem and why. He should also be willing to educate you in basic terms regarding the rationale for his approach to the problem. Finally, it is important to make sure that you ask about price from the very beginning and have clearly written documentation to enforce this understanding.

A wonderful example of this empowering tool can be seen in a client we will call Mary. Mary, who was experiencing her first pregnancy, had a strong desire to deliver her baby naturally, which for her meant not having a preventative IV and working with a medical staff that was fully supportive of facilitating a natural birth process. Fortunately for Mary, she had done her homework. She knew that most hospitals in the nineties advertised labor and delivery rooms that support natural childbirth. She had also read several good books on the subject and knew the questions to ask as she searched for an obstetrician who would support her wishes. To her surprise, she discovered that finding an obstetrician willing to work collaboratively as an equal participant in the process was not as easy as she had thought.

In her first trimester, she was happily complying with her doctor's care until she began to have doubts about his commitment to the process of natural childbirth. We began to explore in the therapy what might be causing these doubts, and I encouraged her to ask her doctor more questions about the process and choices involved. The following week, Mary reported that she had fired him. She was shocked to discover his defensive demeanor when she began to ask more thorough questions. Mary could immediately see that this would not bode well for his willingness to support her choices under the duress of labor pains.

As she shopped for a more supportive doctor, she utilized the technique of interviewing the doctor in the first session. With effort, Mary finally found a birthing center and an obstetrician who respected her wishes and worked with her as an equal partner in the process of childbirth. While this process is not fool proof, it certainly worked for Mary, who reported that the birth of her child was the most profoundly satisfying moment of her life.

It is important to emphasize that identifying the NPD person during the acquaintance stage is difficult. If we are already entangled at the point we make this discovery, the best we may do is seek help from another party, cut our losses, and bail out. Depending on the nature of the business arrangement and the degree of difficult behavior, it can be helpful to consult with outside professionals who have similar expertise, as well as to consult with a support person who may offer helpful coping strategies.

The NPD Client

On the other side of the fence is the importance of recognizing the NPD client when you are in a profession that provides a service. Finding out too late that one of your clients is a narcissist can be costly, not only emotionally, but also financially, and professionally. The narcissist's attitude of entitlement alongside a potentially compromised capacity for ethical behavior can leave you high and dry after investing considerable effort, time, and money.

A recent example of this occurred with an editor who was contracted to ghostwrite a medical book for a doctor who specialized in a particular field of medicine. The process moved forward smoothly for the first six months, but became increasingly difficult as her client began demanding more and more rewrites. In spite of the increasing demands of the doctor, she was able to complete the manuscript and submit it on time. At this point, the doctor and publisher accepted the manuscript in its entirety without requiring any further rewrites or alterations. As far as the editor knew, the project was considered satisfactorily completed, and her client was happy.

When the book was published, the editor received a copy and discovered that her name had been removed from the acknowledgment page. Not only did the doctor refuse to give her credit for her considerable contribution to his book, but he also refused to honor his balance owing, forcing her to take legal action to receive payment for her work.

This example of covert narcissism on the part of the doctor illustrates the importance of ensuring your rights as a service provider through detailed contractual agreement. Most important, her story highlights the necessity of insisting on regular and timely payments for services provided. Holding your client accountable to make regular payments for services as you provide them will keep the narcissist's entitlement in check, as well as his attitude of respect.

The Criminal Narcissist

It must be made clear that the importance of identifying and understanding severe degrees of pathological narcissism is not just for the improved quality of our personal lives. Our very survival as a society and species is most likely dependent on our recognition of unhealthy narcissism and our ability to confront these issues in others and ourselves. We must come to terms with the fact that the human psyche is complicated, and we are obligated to develop psychological understanding beyond simplistic notions of right and wrong or good and evil. Sickness that becomes so twisted it crosses over into "evil" does not fall from the sky like a meteor or materialize in a puff of smoke from other worlds ruled by the devil.

Sickness evolves into evil from innumerable small, subtle, and incremental actions (little lies, if you will), like missing a road sign and then stubbornly refusing to acknowledge that we have gone awry. Likewise, as codependents, we can invest more and more in a relationship that is continually giving us warning signs. With a similar unwillingness to retrace our steps, we ignore the need to re-examine the basic assumptions of what makes an individual capable of a healthy relationship in the first place. No one is more vulnerable to becoming attracted to the narcissist than the codependent, and the narcissist, in turn, is drawn to the codependent. The NPD individual is unfortunately a far more predatory individual than we may want to admit. If we are to utilize our skills as self-reflecting individuals, we must accept these complex and painful realities and empower ourselves to confront them.

Unhealthy narcissism often becomes so pathological it seems indistinguishable from evil. Scott Peck, M.D. wrote eloquently about this fact in his marvelous book, *People of the Lie*. For reasons that I suspect are similar to Scott Peck, I am devoted to this subject. *Narcissism is the last train stop before Hell!* In other words, if we don't confront unhealthy degrees of narcissism in ourselves as well as in others, we may fail to catch a destructive tendency before it does significant damage.

The narcissist who has never been confronted and encouraged to look at himself is vulnerable to acting out his grandiose delusions, inflicting injury on those nearest to him. At times, these are the criminals that we read about in the paper, the ex-employee who returns to his company, takes out a gun, and kills as many people as he can before turning it on himself, or the spouse who kills his partner (and sometimes children) before killing himself. Worse yet, the malignant narcissists are sometimes the teenagers who nurture their hate until they commit horrible acts of violence on their innocent peers. By the time the narcissist crosses the line into unlawful actions, he has fully decided that these actions are justified, regardless of how society might see it. Sometimes the suicide note may even reflect these delusions, expressing a kind of perverted empathy that he killed his wife or children because it would be too cruel to leave them behind.

To be honest with ourselves, we must acknowledge that the human psyche has many dimensions and have the courage to understand and actively confront toxic narcissism on the part of individuals and/or groups. To continue the blame game with simplistic attitudes is to fall into the very arrogance that we need to identify and stop. There are many warning signs of severe narcissism if we would be willing to recognize them.

Most importantly, prevention requires the understanding of healthy child rearing skills that involve recognition and empathy for the true feelings and needs of the child. When we can recognize attitudes and behaviors that reflect unhealthy narcissism, we can become our own gardeners, uprooting these behaviors in ourselves. Similarly, we can prevent others from encroaching into boundaries where they don't belong and assertively redirect an unhealthy path in another person. At the very least, we may recognize the potential for violence that so frequently appears to strike us from nowhere and take preventative action.

The Malignant Narcissist Takes Power— The Nightmare of Group Narcissism

During the final stages of writing this book, the horrifying murder of over three thousand people was master minded by the world's most recent example of the *malignant narcissist*, meaning the uncontrolled and dangerous narcissist, Osama Bin Laden. Previous to this tragic event, I had primarily decided to write about Adolph Hitler due to the fact that he is the most widely known malignant narcissist who has taken power in a modern, technologically advanced society. However, due to the relevance of Bin Laden's destructive capacity in a global community where nations increasingly rely on each other for survival, I have included him in this discussion.

First, let's consider the common histories of these infamous individuals. Both Hitler and Bin Laden had parents with humble roots and autocratic fathers who fought for their legitimacy and good standing. Both fathers ruled their families with an iron fist and a black and white system of child rearing.

With the advantage of time, we know a great deal more about Hitler's childhood than we presently know about Bin Laden. For instance, we know that he was severely abused in the most arbitrary manner possible by his father's nighttime rages when he would awaken the young Adolph, drag him from his bed, and brutally beat him. This unrelenting abuse alongside his mother's passivity and idealization of her husband combined to create a completely distorted version of reality for Hitler. His own repression and idealization of his childhood was well known and even perpetuated for some time after his death by historians reluctant to accept the more disturbing aspects of his early life.

While there is no evidence either way to prove Hitler's ancestry, what is important here is the psychological contribution to the most destructive "repetition compulsion" ever reenacted in history. Hitler's inheritance of shame (from rumors of his father's "illegitimate" birth history) and hatred that he felt towards his father led Hitler to "split off" these feelings, repressing and externalizing them onto others. However, because no individual can succeed in such a mission, he is doomed to a continual reenactment until it collapses from its own destruction. In Hitler's case, his reenactment was taken out on an entire race of people with the Nazi law requiring all German citizens to prove their "pure" heritage three generations back. Those who were Jewish or of Jewish ancestry were then selected for imprisonment and murder. Later, Hitler's need for more victims led to the extension of this policy to many other groups deemed to be impure.

From adolescence on, the young Adolph sought to reshape himself as the representative of a superior race, his grandiose self-image emerging directly from his unconscious experience of self as shameful, inferior, and helpless. It was no accident that he picked two groups that represented both his shame and his helplessness, those who were Jewish (targets for the shame he felt from his questionable heritage) and those who represented the helplessness of his childhood (the mentally retarded and infirm of society). These people literally became the first victims that he rounded up for the incomprehensible intention of "extermination." In other words, the sociopath-narcissist seeks to re-enact the murder of his own psyche, now from the perspective of the perpetrator.

Finally, in choosing the Jews as his scapegoat, Hitler found a convenient target for the envy underlying his narcissism and the narcissism of his followers. You will remember that envy is the primary conscious feeling that drives the NPD individual to compete and surpass those whom he regards as more powerful and/or successful. The sociopath-narcissist will obsessively focus on those individuals, groups, or nations who represent the pinnacle of power and success, devising and conspiring ways to overthrow them. Just as Hitler demonstrated with his book, *Mein Kampf*, Bin Laden also made no secret of his intentions to destroy the United States, progressively vilifying all Americans whom he saw as the source of "Muslim shame."

Bin Laden's father also made his mark in the world with a single-minded purpose to succeed and to enforce a rigid discipline on his fifty-two children, Osama Bin Laden being the seventeenth son. Little imagination is required to grasp how difficult it might be to achieve the normal narcissistic needs of feeling valued and important in a sibling set of fifty-two. While we know that Bin Laden's father was a rigid disciplinarian and a strict enforcer of religious teachings and behavior, we do not know the unique daily circumstances of his life growing up. Regardless, as these facts are known, they will undoubtedly shed more light on how Bin Laden's personality was shaped, leaving him vulnerable to become the sociopath terrorist of today.

One point is clear. There is a stark contrast between the rigid constrictions on his freedom as a child and becoming the heir of millions at the age of twelve when his father died suddenly in a plane crash. We can easily visualize how Bin Laden may be reenacting his history when we hear reports depicting him surrounded by followers like children at his feet. He then exhorts these same followers to "win glory" for themselves by becoming human bombs in hijacked planes.

Some facts do reveal that Bin Laden has wished to compete with the revered figure of his father. We have learned from anonymous sources that when Saddam Hussein invaded Kuwait, Bin Laden was anxious to prove his loyalty to Saudi Arabia by fighting to protect the Saudi borders. It is reported that he felt a great sense of depression when the

United States took the lead role in this war. We also know that this was the turning point that focused his hatred towards the United States.

If we consider the narcissist's need to achieve greatness, we can see how his grandiose plans to surpass his father's heroic status were shattered by the US and betrayed by the people of his country for allowing the US to usurp his intended role. In addition, this break with his home country allowed Bin Laden to express the unbridled hatred and envy towards the United States, the scapegoat for his internal experience of self as insignificant or inadequate. As with Hitler, it is Bin Laden's envy and desire for revenge that ultimately drove him to topple the World Trade Towers—the unmistakable symbol of economic superiority in the very heart of America's greatest city. The ideology of extreme Muslim fundamentalism, like the extreme ideologies of any other fanatical group, simply becomes the convenient framework for the malignant narcissist to express his boundless hatred and desire for revenge.

Both Hitler and Bin Laden, however, beg a far more important question. How do such sick and destructive individuals become legitimized and endorsed by entire nations or masses of people throughout the world? We can see on the surface that the malignant narcissist in power is an individual who uses his charisma and intelligence to inflate an ideology among a group of people who are vulnerable to blindly follow, no matter how irrational the claims appear to be. Members of both the Nazi Aryan supremacists and the extreme Muslim fundamentalists foster the delusion that their people are the only "true" people—believing that everyone else must meet their test of conformity or be destroyed.

When we look at the axis nations that were drawn into the fascist movements of World War II or the terrorists who follow Bin Laden, we see important clues about the shared traits of these diverse groups. Each of these nations and groups have had strong tendencies towards group conformity alongside a severe tendency to idealize their beliefs to the point of grandiosity—a dynamic that Alice Miller, in her book, *For Your Own Good*, terms "poisonous pedagogy."

Most importantly, Alice Miller brings the issue down to each and every family raising a child and the degree of unconscious narcissistic wounding that exists. A cultural mindset that leads to child-rearing practices that ignore the thoughts and feelings of the child and emphasize blind obedience are the very conditions that make a group of people vulnerable to fascist movements. While American baby-boomers have often been criticized for being spoiled by an overindulgent parenting style, this same group is highly individualistic and diverse in composition, unlikely to become seduced by a lock step mentality of destructive conformity.

However, lest we become too self-satisfied, we should not forget that we have our own dark periods in history when our self-righteous beliefs led to such feelings of superiority that we justified our oppression and ravaging of Native Americans and African Americans. We also see in the McCarthy era, a mere fifty years ago, an example of the paranoia that is so often combined with severe narcissism. Finally, the painful period of the Vietnam war has perhaps matured us as a nation with the recognition that our previous perspective on the world had become archaic, and we, too, could fall into the error of trying to justify the continuance of a questionable war.

Perhaps one of the more insidious forms of group narcissism occurs among the CEOs and vice-presidents of many modern corporations around the globe. Hidden behind the boardroom doors, we often learn too late how profit-hunting groups make decisions with impunity that ravage the health or finances of unsuspecting individuals or ruin the precious resources of our planet. These groups reflect all the dynamics of covert narcissism and have less and less accountability for their actions, a dangerous combination for the well being of everyone.

The following dynamics are universally shared by groups of people developing severe narcissistic tendencies. These tendencies in turn foster an attitude of righteous justification for the destructive and domineering behaviors towards other groups or nations.

- Child rearing practices that emphasize rigid conformity and unquestioning obedience to the beliefs of the parents.
- Over-emphasis on conformity and an intolerance of diversity in society at large.
- Grandiose ideology—self-righteousness of one's beliefs as superior over others.

- Tendencies towards paranoia (i.e., censorship of opposing opinions).

- An inability to engage in a rational dialogue that acknowledges the rights of others.

- Over simplistic thinking: all or nothing, black or white thinking.

When we add in social chaos and a history of demoralization due to the existence of war and/or economic depression (as we see in Germany following World War I and Afghanistan following twenty years of war), the ideal set of conditions exists for the malignant narcissist to rise to power.

On the codependent side of the coin, many individuals in England and America were similarly blinded by their righteous attachment to their "pacifist" ideologies—to such a point that they could not recognize the inevitable danger to their own free society. Like the entrenched codependent with the NPD individual, these groups regularly called for soul searching and an ever-increasing intention to reason with Hitler to prevent conflict. Caught up in a stubborn denial, the pacifists were unable to recognize the important warning signs of malignant narcissism gathering strength in an entire nation of people.

An excellent character who reflects the dangers of inverted narcissism (severe codependency) is the lord of the English manor in the film, *Remains of the Day.* As host to the German Nazi "ambassadors" visiting under the false pretense of engaging in a dialogue for peace, he is so absorbed in his own ideology and principles that he doesn't see that the Nazi's are using him. While he rigidly adheres to his ideology for peaceful coexistence, the German ambassadors are quietly taking inventory of the valuables in the manor home—property they intend to steal after they have taken power.

Our own country seems at times to hang dangerously in the balance as the unwieldy size of our governing bodies and corporations leave the empowerment of the individual behind. Caught by an increasing sense of alienation and hopelessness, we could fall prey to the insidious tendency to hand over power to the narcissist leader or group that promises to deliver a shiny new sense of individuality—a potential impostor of our true ideals.

Encounters with the narcissist and the malignant narcissist force us to recognize the lesson that we need to learn most—that human existence is complex, and we must accept responsibility for this complexity. We cannot have simplistic answers and solutions to our lives, nor can we complacently rely on old formulas that may have once guided our choices. Toxic narcissism exists in the shadows, often remaining invisible until revealed by the pain it causes others. If we are to prevent these dangers, we must become more psychologically sophisticated, working through our own narcissistic tendencies and proactively drawing the line on abusive tendencies in other individuals, groups, and potential world leaders.

CHAPTER SEVEN SUMMARY

The NPD friendship relationship

The same dynamics we have been discussing between the NPD individual and others will occur within the friendship relationship, as you become insidiously drawn into the codependent pattern of giving and supporting with little exchange on the part of the NPD person. You can discover the degree of healthy or unhealthy narcissism by exploring your friend's ability to reciprocate in the give and take of support and assistance. You may also investigate her ability to talk through an *issue* that might come up. If you recognize the dynamics of narcissism in a friendship relationship, you will need to work on asserting effective boundaries in self-care. Efforts to increase your ability to assert your thoughts, feelings, and needs, as well as to maintain healthy boundaries, will cause you to struggle with the deeper issues that underlie your codependency issues. When you are able to recognize your strengths and assert an equal exchange in friendship relationships, you will gain a sense of freedom and self-esteem that is well worthwhile and inspires your momentum towards your own goals.

The NPD individual in the workplace

The NPD person in the workplace will have a tendency to create havoc among his peers and simultaneously rise to a position of power because he flourishes in a competitive environment. Some of the warning signals that you may notice are:

NPD person's behaviors:	Codependent's responses:
● Cannot acknowledge you for a job well done	● Feel emotionally drained after interactions
● Takes recognition you deserve	● Increasing tendency to doubt yourself
● Absorbs your time, energy and attention with his/her agenda	● Feel unclear about expectations
● Undermines your competence in front of others	● Become less and less focused on your goals and work agenda
● Subtly or not so subtly prevents your advancement	● Increasing feelings of frustration, resentment, anxiety, and powerlessness
● Sends double messages and resists clarifying matters of performance	● "Burnout," an inability for self-care, making decisions, or changing your job circumstances
● Sets you up as scapegoat	

Boundary setting skills with the narcissist is equal to self-preservation when it comes to your career, and the potential negative impact to your self-esteem. Survival tactics for coping with the narcissist include the following:

- Set limits on listening time and rehearse exit strategies.
- Limit praise and support.
- Limit offering your expertise and ideas beyond what is necessary.
- Prepare for change-back defenses through mental and emotional rehearsal.
- Be alert to your guilt response and maintain your self-preservation measures.
- Find a "safe" outside support person who you can talk to.
- Keep a daily log of your work activities.
- Write memos of all meetings, changes to plans, or matters related to your performance.
- Send copies to other people involved.
- When under threat of the NPD person's devaluing agenda have a third party present at all significant interactions.
- Find another position, if necessary, preferably before being fired.
- Be proactive.

The NPD service provider

As in the work environment, you may find yourself unwittingly involved in a professional relationship with an NPD person. To prevent getting stuck, always interview a prospective service provider by asking for plenty of information:

- How he will approach meeting your needs.
- Why he would choose that approach.
- How he will handle delays and problems.
- Explanation of basic terms.
- Written estimate of costs.

If the potential service provider becomes defensive, impatient, angry, or continues to evade the specifics, you may have important indicators that this person is more interested in his own agenda than meeting your needs. While the interview process is not fool proof, you dramatically increase your ability to surface unhealthy narcissism that might be present.

The NPD client

The same tools of interviewing and clarifying agreements that will be put into writing are necessary from the other side of the relationship if you are the service provider. Making sure that your client is accountable for his/her payments for your services in a timely fashion will ensure against being burned financially and command a greater sense of respect in general from a potential NPD client.

The Narcissist in Society

The criminal narcissist

More and more, we are witnessing the frightening and tragic results that occur when a narcissist crosses the line into criminal behavior. As responsible citizens of society, we need to recognize toxic narcissism in others so that we can set limits and help redirect the path of an NPD individual before he becomes emboldened to act out his rage.

The malignant narcissist in power

At the extreme end of the continuum, we see what happens when the malignant narcissist takes power. These individuals often begin as the charismatic autocratic leader who can influence masses of people to abuse and violate the rights and/or boundaries of other groups or nations. As free thinkers in a democratic society, we must learn to recognize and resist unhealthy narcissism in others and ourselves if we are to avoid and prevent the toxic and infectious nature of such movements.

CHAPTER EIGHT

There's No Place Like Home!

The Shared Road to Recovery

Falling Asleep and Sleepwalking

Dorothy's journey through Oz begins as she is knocked unconscious in a storm and wakes in her bed with no awareness of where she is or how she got there. A wonderful metaphor for the unconscious state of early adult life, the goal for Dorothy and for us is to find our way home to claim our true selves. Agonizing over which road to take, Dorothy encounters one set of difficulties after another and sets her hopes on the grand illusion of Oz. Her innocence and lack of vigilance cause her one delay after another, and she becomes more vulnerable to the dangers of evildoers. She is as they say—"an easy mark."

Of course, Dorothy is fated to become entangled with the illusions of Oz, each one teaching her something about life, courage, and her own strengths. Rich in symbolism, Dorothy finally discovers that Oz is an impostor, and that she has always had the power to return home. At the end of your own journey with a narcissistic individual, you, too, have come to learn that toxic narcissism in a person is both seductive and disguised, an enticing invitation into an unreal world.

With a surface presentation that is often captivating, we are drawn to the narcissist. Initially our feelings of attraction, admiration, or intimidation become the emotional state that holds us spellbound. Eventually, however, the negative influences of the narcissist erode our trust and confidence inducing a state of emotional paralysis. And the length of time that we struggle to find our way out of the narcissist's world can vary from days—to years—to a whole lifetime. Let's recap what the dangers of toxic narcissism are all about.

You will remember that the word narcissism in general means "self-worship." Consequently, unhealthy narcissism is a form of claiming too much for the self, whether we are taking resources from others, or indulging in too much pride in our talents or achievements. Perhaps we have had fortunate circumstances in business, family position, beauty, or other inherent gifts from God or the natural world. While healthy narcissism *does* involve our ability to feel proud of special accomplishments and to take pleasure in our abilities, we generally know that heady feeling when we indulge in undue pride, a tendency that leads to self-aggrandizement. The moment we claim more credit for ourselves than we deserve, we participate in the illusion of "special ownership" or "entitlement" and head towards the dead-end of toxic narcissism.

In the end, the constant pursuit of maintaining a presentation that is "larger than life," whether it is talent, beauty, achievement, or some other quality, leaves us empty, unfulfilled, and yearning for something more. Like the Wizard in his castle, the narcissist eventually becomes a prisoner of his own defenses, disconnected and alone.

Dorothy illustrates the journey of the codependent person who becomes enthralled with the grandeur of Oz, seeking to find her worth and power by gaining his approval and help. Although she is capable of intimacy (as we see in her friendships with her three companions), she is unable to recognize her true strengths and abilities.

Similarly, if you suffer from codependency issues, your own unmet needs for self-worth may cause you to be attracted to individuals with strong narcissistic traits. The more you examine your feelings, the more you may uncover the unconscious pledge that goes something like this: "If I give my very best, if I give my 'all,' then he or she will be there for me when my turn comes." This unspoken, but powerful oath allows you to ignore the many clues that reflect the profound limitations of the narcissist. Only *when you "hit bottom" and recognize his or her inability to be there for you, will you begin to face the changes you need to make in yourself and your relationship.* These dynamics of codependency and narcissism can occur in the context of almost any type of relationship: co-worker, friend, family, or love relationship.

At times, the narcissistic dynamic can be so camouflaged and insidious that even a healthy bystander may fall prey to her need for participants, admirers, support people, and givers. In short, anyone may be vulnerable to the seductive illusions of another person's narcissism. By the time you realize the one-way nature of the relationship, the destruction and erosion to your self-esteem can be devastating. In addition, you may have developed a profound devotion to your role as the NPD person's indispensable care taker and simultaneously feel an emotional desperation for acceptance, approval, or love from the narcissist. This pattern can become so entrenched that you develop an equally powerful system of denial and inability to recognize your own "false self." In chapter six, we discussed the complementary defenses of the codependent as the larger than life care taker of others.

The Quest for Self-awareness

If you have codependency issues, your own narcissistic injuries are manifested through low self-esteem and an inability to recognize the very real strengths that you possess. Just as Dorothy cannot make use of the power that is literally at her feet, we cannot make use of our inner gifts until we can claim with confidence that we have these natural abilities.

Imagine living out your life on a meager patch of land covered with weeds. All the while you are unaware that just inches beneath the dirt are the riches of a gold mine. For all practical purposes, the abundance of wealth easily within reach does not exist. Like Dorothy, perhaps we have to learn the hard way. Dorothy came perilously close to being burned alive before she could wake up to the fact that she had been chasing an illusion. For the same reasons, we must see past the impressive show of the NPD individual and penetrate our own false beliefs before we can recognize our capacity and birthright for love. Our courage to confront the illusions of toxic narcissism will come from some painful moment that helps us break free and see the hidden truth under the surface. Finally, we may need to explore and test our abilities before we are ready to see the truth about *ourselves*.

If you are presently in a relationship with a narcissistic person, you will need to develop awareness and confidence in your feelings, choices, and abilities before you can clear up your confusion about the relationship. Your biggest trap is probably fear—fear of the unknown. Fear may provoke you to continually excuse the NPD person and to doubt yourself. You may choose to keep your head in the sand, fearful of what it might mean if you recognize the depth of the problem.

Consequently, your first ally is knowledge about healthy and unhealthy narcissism. The more you know, the less you will fear. With knowledge and understanding, you will be able to stand your ground when the NPD individual puts you on the defensive. Eventually, you must face the truth about the deteriorating impact that this relationship is having on your life. *Until you recognize that your avoidance of the problems in this relationship only contributes to more losses, you will likely stay in your comfort zone no matter how unsatisfied you feel.*

It is no coincidence that the cowardly lion in Oz turned out to be the most narcissistic of Dorothy's three friends. Enveloped by fear, Lion is continually requiring the attention and support of Dorothy and her two friends. In a similar way, the more codependent we become in our relationship with the narcissist, the more we require and often demand of friends and family to stay at baseline functioning. Before we know it, we become more narcissistic and self-absorbed in a complementary fashion to the narcissist.

Confronting the Impostor

Dorothy had to explore many twists and turns in the road before she had the courage to make her first discovery—*Oz was an impostor.* With her new skills, she overcomes her fear and confronts Oz for his unfair treatment and broken promises. At last she holds her ground with the intimidating image on the projection screen. Here we see the parallels to the narcissist's primary defense of projection—a tactic that puts the recipient immediately on the defense.

Recognizing the defense of projection is a powerful tool in dealing with individuals or groups that have severe narcissism. To recognize and block the impact of a projection, you must have a clear understanding how this defense operates and be able to recognize how your own or another person's unconscious feelings may play out in the dynamic of a projection. Let's return to the fact that the NPD individual is unable to recognize her negative feelings and problems. And remember, too, negative feelings don't disappear simply because we do not want to deal with them—they, in fact, become more intense.

Because the NPD individual is so unconscious of her feelings, she invariably projects these negative feelings and qualities onto others. Consciously, she feels justified to vent her anger and criticism towards these unwanted traits in someone else—primarily those closest to her. Finally, the narcissist will often project these unconscious feelings with all the fervor of a crusader, a force that can hold you hostage as you fall into the trap of defending yourself. When you can identify her projections and let go of your need to defend yourself, you will be free to claim your own inner gifts and strengths.

Letting go means giving up the search for recognition or acceptance from the NPD person. By now, you are perhaps realizing that the more you persist in defending yourself, the more you erode your self-esteem. Eventually, you must come to terms with the fact that the NPD person may be unable see you. She is generally seeing only her projected image of you alongside her determination for you to conform to this image. The painful truth you must reconcile is her inability to acknowledge you for yourself.

Often, in an ironic twist, the narcissist projects some form of her inability to give onto the codependent person. Perhaps you have been accused of not being understanding, emotionally generous, or supportive. Although you may think you can easily see through such false statements, your actions to defend yourself only increase your sensitivity to such accusations. After all, giving to and caring for others may be a primary strength, therefore, an important source of self-esteem.

In an effort to prove her wrong, you may strive even harder to be giving and supportive. Meanwhile, you are furthering the denial of your angry, resentful emotions. Ultimately, you may become caught in a web of compromise, sacrificing a genuine relationship for one that offers financial reward, "legitimacy," or other forms of security. The most painful irony is that you may end up with no security at all when the time comes to confront the truth about your relationship.

Discovering the truth about ourselves, our thoughts, feelings, and desires is our greatest step towards growth. When we earnestly search for the truth of our feelings, we will be ready to respond to the projections of the narcissist. As you see past the false projections and set limits on the "entitlement" behaviors, you are free to pursue genuine respect, friendship, and love. You are also free to discover if your NPD parent, lover, spouse, friend, or colleague is capable of meeting you half way. Dorothy initiated her discovery by angrily confronting Oz for his unfair treatment. At the same time, her dog Toto exposes the impostor by pulling back the curtain. Free from the projections and lies, she is able to reject Oz's commands. Now she must face the anger she feels towards Oz for duping and exploiting her for so long.

Rediscovering the Self and Emotional Healing

In spite of the tepid portrayal of Dorothy's anger, we nevertheless do witness her feelings as she chastises the little man for being such an impostor. A more accurate reflection of the codependent's anger would be seen by Luke Skywalker, dueling with his father, Darth Vader, and struggling not to give in to hate. Skywalker's *rage* is generally closer to the truth for anyone who has been burned in a relationship with the NPD individual. In fact, resolving these feelings of anger is one of the primary tasks in the healing process. You may remember from chapter five that there are generally three tasks involved in resolving such intense negative feelings.

The first task is to recognize and acknowledge your anger. If you have codependency issues, you may need help from an outside support person to come to terms with the truth of your angry feelings—primarily because you have significant defenses that cause you to repress and suppress these feelings. We must acknowledge our feelings of anger, even rage, for the unfair nature of such a relationship. Here, too, we encounter our profound feelings of fear—fear of what our angry feelings may mean.

The second task of healing is resolving the anger and hurt through a constructive process that will help you to release these feelings. You will need to express your feelings in a safe setting with a support person who can validate and empathize with you—not minimize your experiences or try to *"fix it"* for you. A trusted (healthy) friend, mental health professional, or sponsor in a twelve-step program is generally a vital part of this process. In contrast to the immediate resolution we see for Dorothy and her friends, reconciling our negative feelings of hurt, anger, or fear takes longer than a single moment of insight or a one-time opportunity to ventilate.

We must take the time we need to untangle the many hurts and betrayals we feel with the NPD person. We must also recognize that much of our anger is due to the self-critical feelings we harbor for being "so blind" or for "wasting so much time." Invariably, we begin to recognize that our own history (including childhood history) shaped the vulnerabilities that led to our self-sabotaging patterns of behavior. *As we compassionately come to terms with the truth of our deeper feelings and experiences from childhood, we learn empathy for ourselves.* In turn, this empathy helps us let go of the anger we feel with the narcissist.

Like our heroine, Dorothy, in *The Wizard of Oz*, we receive far too many messages from our culture that we should be able to achieve the quick fix once we have identified the problem. We believe that we should just "get over it," or we naively wish that insight alone would transform us overnight. Consequently, we tend to short-change the importance, determination, and patience needed for the whole journey, especially the emotional healing stage.

Empowerment

The third task is empowerment. Rich in metaphor, Dorothy and her friends transform before our very eyes as they confidently embrace the gifts that change their beliefs. In a similar fashion, we really do have the ability to overcome our self-limiting false notions and, in turn, to set limits on the distorted expectations of others. *We can become the people we long to become.* However, let's remember again. Quick fixes don't happen in life! The final leg of the journey involves changing your internalized false beliefs by setting boundaries that command a more self-respecting relationship with the narcissist and others in general.

Codependent behavior is a form of passivity, over-accommodating, internalizing feelings of anger, and a tendency towards self-doubt. Few of us can behave assertively by simply learning a prescribed set of responses and then doing them. We generally need coaching, lots of practice, and plenty of patience and perseverance. Books on assertiveness such as Harriett Lerner's, *The Dance of Anger*, or Anne Katherine's *Where to Draw the Line*, and many others can help you learn your own style of assertiveness that fits best for you. In the end we can only arrive at our destination when we put our new awareness to the test. *Consequently it is our new behaviors that bring a fuller and healthier "experience of self." Insight and emotional healing must be anchored in new behaviors that reflect our changing perspective.*

Perhaps there is one event in *The Wizard of Oz* where our analogy to the narcissist breaks down—the transformation of Oz into a kind, wise, father figure who helps Dorothy and her friends recognize the resources they already have. In reality, we cannot expect the NPD individual to assist us in validating our own strengths. On the contrary, we must discover these strengths through other people and supportive environments.

Yet, if we view the little man behind the curtain as taking a kind of narcissistic credit for the accomplishments that Dorothy and her friends had already achieved, perhaps this part of the story is an apt metaphor after all. Sometimes the NPD person will try to take credit for another person's transformation, pretending that he deliberately behaved poorly so that she could grow. Regardless of how we interpret this part of the story, we can be sure that we will move backwards and forwards on the path of growth as we struggle with insight, emotional healing, and the assertiveness skills of boundary setting. We will require many opportunities to test our wings and plenty of support from individuals who can validate our efforts.

The empowerment stage of the journey involves understanding and negotiating healthy boundaries in a relationship. In chapters one through three, we talked about the powerful pull that narcissistic individuals can exert, causing you to lose sight of your own boundaries and sense of self in the relationship. We also discussed the importance of recognizing reciprocal efforts that exist in healthy relationships. If you are involved with a person who has the full narcissistic disorder, you will experience what is best epitomized in an analogy to a black hole—an area in outer space so powerful that everything around it is sucked in, including light.

The black hole is the ultimate archetype of the one-way relationship with the narcissist.

Many clients I have with worked over the years have referred to the "black hole" as they struggle to describe their relationships with the NPD person. Most of the giving that you do in the relationship seems to disappear into the void, rarely reciprocated, and often unacknowledged. So, too, like the black hole, the force field surrounding the narcissist is invisible and powerful—a treacherous trap to the innocent traveler. This analogy also pertains to the strategy that you will need to protect yourself. Your primary protection is to know where the perimeter or boundary is, map your course safely, and prevent yourself from being drawn in. *Consequently, if you take one thing away from this book, it would be the ability to recognize unhealthy narcissism, set boundaries, and learn the assertiveness skills for maintaining them.*

You will need to take risks, assert your rights and opinions, and discover your strengths. Only time will reveal the narcissistic person's true character and ability for self-reflection and change. While the full picture of a person is always a complex one, we can be on the lookout for another person's capacity for give-and-take. Most of us realize we cannot expect to have everything we want in a relationship with another person. But we can expect a reasonable exchange of thoughts, feelings, and other resources when both parties are capable of healthy boundaries and empathy for others.

In the final analysis, we must assert our needs and set limits on unrealistic expectations if we want to be released from the resentment that occurs in a one-way relationship. Even when we know we cannot penetrate the narcissist's defenses, we feel much better about ourselves when we set limits on the NPD individual's destructive behaviors and insist that he or she share more responsibility for the relationship. As we boldly step out of our codependent agreements that revolve around caretaking the NPD person, we revitalize our energy and restore an optimistic outlook on life.

In the conclusion of *The Wizard of Oz*, we are also given insight about what happens for the narcissist. Floating off in his balloon, he is indeed a kinder, gentler version of a narcissist, yet he remains in his own world as he disappears into the distance. Although we may achieve a softer and more respectful relationship with the narcissist, we may never achieve the deep and rich connection that is possible with a healthier individual.

Regardless of the NPD person's capacity for change, your own growth and assertiveness efforts will reduce the degree of toxic narcissism in this relationship whether it is a co-worker, friend, family member, or partner, transforming the relationship to a more benign coexistence. You may even see the beginnings of genuine growth. In the worst-case scenario, you may be forced to recognize that the NPD person is incapable of change as he remains unable to recognize your feelings, and unrelenting in his effort to control the resources of attention, support, empathy, and other resources. Your courageous efforts to face the truth about this relationship before you allow more months and years to pass will prevent the inevitable damage from an increased sense of loss.

Unfortunately, we are not able to continue with the story of Dorothy and her friends to see how it turns out as they carry on with their lives. We cannot know how difficult their struggle really is as they practice using their new gifts. We might imagine that they will need continued support such as coaching, mentoring, and encouragement. We can also imagine that Lion may have awkward and uncertain moments as he "incarnates" into his new courageous self. Scarecrow may stumble as he goes out into the world to share his knowledge. Tin Man may even have a disastrous relationship as he learns about his ability to love. And Dorothy may find that she wishes to make serious alterations in her life as she recognizes her true desires and abilities.

Whatever we might envision for Dorothy, Scarecrow, Tin Man, and Lion, we can be sure that they will continue to face and wrestle with old internalized doubts and fears. Along with our friends in the story, we, too, will struggle on the path towards greater fulfillment in life. Yet our commitment to the healing journey allows us to reclaim a life of authenticity and to experience the deep satisfaction that Dorothy feels when she says, "There's no place like home!"

CHAPTER EIGHT SUMMARY

The specific nature of your relationship with someone who has strong issues with narcissism, as well as the degree of emotional pain it causes, will determine the type of help you may need in dealing with this person. Yet, in all the different types of relationships, you will find the steps towards a healthier balance of give-and-take the same:

- Recognize the dimensions of unhealthy narcissism in your relationship and validate the destructive impact on your life and your sense of self.

- Identify your own history of "unfinished emotional business" that causes you to be vulnerable to the one-way relationships of narcissistic individuals.

- Seek support for healing your own narcissistic wounding that has led to issues of codependency.

- Develop the ability to recognize healthy boundaries and assertive limit setting.

- Practice letting go of unhealthy narcissism in yourself and your relationships so that you can fulfill your own deeper potential.

Allow yourself the ongoing support system that you may need to manifest these changes over time.

APPENDIX

Looking in Your Own Backyard

Resources for Treatment

Self-help groups

One of the most powerful tools for healing can be seen in the various twelve-step self-help programs originally developed for helping people with addictions and later extended to assist people with emotional and behavioral compulsions of all kinds. My hope is that a twelve-step program will be developed for dealing with the issues of toxic narcissism and codependency in individuals who are in relationship with NPD people. Because addiction so powerfully parallels the dynamics of unhealthy narcissism, these groups often address toxic narcissism and codependency to narcissism without directly addressing the issue of narcissism itself.

Bill Wilson and Dr. Bob, two men with an uncanny instinct for understanding the importance of boundaries, created the original model for the twelve-step program of AA (Alcoholics Anonymous). In their Twelve Traditions (the founding tenets) they spelled out the ground rules that prevented any one person or organization from dominating the process at AA meetings and disallowed AA groups from receiving money or other forms of support from outside individuals or groups. These ground rules not only provide safety for the process of self-disclosure, but also ensure against the narcissism that invariably develops as groups become "institutionalized." In addition, these traditions prevent an individual from imposing his or her thoughts onto another person. In a well-run twelve-step meeting, there is no place for feedback—only listening.

These operational principles seem to be responsible for twelve-step programs maintaining a remarkable degree of integrity over time. Perhaps when groups are vigilant in their prevention against the domination of one person or organization, they also prevent the corruption that comes with individuals or groups striving for power, recognition, influence, status, control, etc. Invariably, when I hear about twelve-step groups with problems and dysfunctional dynamics, these tenets are not being adhered to and boundaries have been blurred.

The recovery process also involves an active engagement of self-reflection that is based on the psychological and spiritual values of honesty, ownership of problems, and maintaining the discipline of boundaries. Consequently, twelve-step groups set the stage for each person to develop awareness of his or her own feelings as well as awareness of the feelings of others. Finally, the twelve steps are an action plan for changing one's attitudes and behaviors. Individuals with strong issues of narcissism or codependency have a much harder time avoiding their destructive tendencies in recovery groups where self-examination and honesty are the primary focus of discussion.

Codependency recovery groups address the ways in which the codependent person becomes entangled in an over focus on others (originally an over focus on the addicted person). However, a primary problem in addressing issues of codependency is the difficulty with the inherent issues of "covert narcissism." The hidden aspects of covert narcissism in codependency often get lost and remain unidentified because they are more difficult to identify. In fact, as we discussed in chapter six, codependency, when taken to an extreme in a person, can become the equivalent to the issues of the covert narcissist.

Regardless of the direction we take for surviving our wounding, we can all be potential candidates for becoming narcissistic—whether overt or covert in nature. So far, twelve-step programs may be less effective in helping codependent individuals face their own issues with narcissistic wounding and grandiose strivings. Melody Beattie and Anne Schaef are two authors who have keen insight into these dynamics and point the way towards healing the issues of self that underlie codependency.

Finally, twelve-step programs are some of the most effective means for confronting a person's issues with denial, the psychological under-pinning that contributes to the problem of addiction and codependency. Like the disease of alcoholism, unhealthy narcissism and its codependent counterpart are protected by powerful systems of denial that prevent the person from recognizing the negative impact of his or her behaviors on others or one's self.

Support people—friends, family members, sponsors, colleagues

Supportive individuals with the capacity to listen, validate, and sepa-rate their own personal agenda from the process of being there for you, can be invaluable on your journey towards growth and change. Confi-dentiality is also vital. While trusted friends in your social and professional arenas can be important support people, you must be will-ing to test the waters by going slowly. Pay attention over a period of time to see whether or not the person you are confiding in has the ability to maintain integrity through confidentiality and can listen in a nonjudgmental way.

Initially, your issues with codependency or narcissism may make it difficult for you to discern a healthy individual. In fact, you may dis-cover that a number of friends or family whom you thought were in your corner are unable to remain supportive as you move towards growth and change. Your own courage to heal and grow becomes too challeng-ing, even threatening, for these individuals to stay with you in the process. If you feel a sense of sabotage from these former allies, it is time for new boundary setting and a reevaluation of your degree of involvement. Consequently, seeking help outside your network of friends and family may be imperative. A cautionary tale here is the number of times that I have seen codependent individuals detach and disengage from one NPD person only to become entangled with another. This is often true for codependent spouses seeking a divorce. With frightening predictability there is a tendency for the codependent person to entrust herself into the hands of an NPD attorney, now adding to the painful consequences that result from poor representation in the divorce process.

Therapists and spiritual counselors

Therapists and clergy are like anybody else; they are subject to their own issues with codependency and narcissism that have invariably caused them to go into the field of helping others as a form of life work. Consequently you will need to discern if these individuals are healthy and have completed the majority of their own healing work before they attempt to help you. Without this safeguard, a helping professional will be prone to acting out his or her unconscious issues within the context of helping his or her "clients." Alice Miller, in her powerful and classic book, *Drama of the Gifted Child*, devotes the entire first chapter to the importance of a therapist doing his or her own healing work. This book may offer some important insights that can help you evaluate the relative health of a therapist or clergy person. The following are several precautions that would be wise to take before you invest your trust in a professional counselor.

There are generally three ways to ensure whether or not you are enlisting a competent professional to help you in your process of healing:

1. Obtain referrals and references from professionals that you have known over time and whose judgment you can trust. (This is, of course, not foolproof, as I have sometimes discovered that referrals from colleagues or other professionals are not always the best choice.)

2. Interview the individual over the phone. If the professional still passes muster, then allow for at least one face-to-face session before making a commitment to the relationship for further counseling. During the first session or two, the helping professional should be able to:

- Be a good listener.
- Offer an understandable explanation as to how he or she would assist you with your problem and why.
- Demonstrate his or her credentials and have physical evidence of them in his or her office.
- Inform you about his or her fee structure and billing process.

- Remain sensitive and respectful, demonstrating awareness that the first session or two in particular is a two-way interviewing process.
- Be open and non-defensive when you ask questions about how he or she would approach helping you with your problem.
- Demonstrate integrity with professional boundaries.
- Remain alert to how much self-disclosure a therapist may offer. (Anything other than a very brief and general willingness to self-disclose may be a warning sign that this person does not have healthy boundaries.)

3. Gain a second opinion to compare and contrast the information and help that you are seeking.

At any point in the process, if you are feeling that your therapist/counselor is not understanding or validating your own feelings and experience, it is imperative to work this through to your satisfaction; otherwise, the therapy relationship could become a destructive one.

Another misunderstanding that exists is the fact that we should be able to complete all our healing work with one therapist or spiritual counselor. By contrast, we may need to recognize that we can accomplish important degrees of healing with a particular therapist and allow ourselves to seek a professional with different strengths if we cannot make the gains we need in a particular therapy relationship. I am not proposing that an individual should attend more than one individual therapy at the same time or jump from one therapy to another prematurely.

Often, unconscious issues that are being stirred up in the therapy process will generate the impulse to quit therapy. It is important to struggle with your doubts openly with your therapist to discover whether or not your difficulties are due to defenses that are activated by the healing process. If you cannot resolve a problematic issue with a given therapist, you may need to get a second opinion to help you decide whether or not to continue. In addition, if you engage in more than one individual therapy at the same time, you may be diluting and/or sabotaging the effectiveness of both therapies.

The only exceptions for attending more than one psychological therapy at the same time would be combining individual therapy with relationship or family therapy (again, my bias is that this should be done with separate therapists) or individual therapy with group therapy (this can be with the same therapist). The important role of boundaries will continue to be a vital part of your healing work no matter what combination of therapies you rely upon. As a client, and, therefore, as a consumer, you would do well to ask the opinion of several therapists when you are curious or doubtful about a particular therapy approach or program.

Coaching

Coaching can also be an invaluable tool for certain needs, particularly support and guidance to actualize your goals. The field of coaching is one of the newest support services on the market, and you will need to be a very astute consumer. Only in the last year has an organizational body (International Coach Federation) been formed to set some standards with regard to training and experience that will allow individuals to be "certified" as a coach. At the moment, almost anyone can represent themselves as a coach and charge fees for this service.

With this in mind, you will want to educate yourself as to the type of coaching you are looking for and find an individual who has the qualifications to help you. Many therapists are branching into this type of work as a subset of what they do and may offer a variety of types of coaching. Coaches may also come from a variety of backgrounds, such as teaching, the business world, engineering, and almost any type of work. Coaching ranges from "executive coaching" to coaching individuals with attention deficit disorder to life enhancement coaching, etc.

The process of coaching is generally done by phone three times a month and includes evaluating your priorities, setting goals, and working on the obstacles that might come up in realizing these goals. From this description, you can probably see how easy it would be for a coach to venture into emotional territory that would at times be better handled in a therapy relationship. Consequently, the issue of boundaries again becomes an important one so that you remain alert to a coach exploring emotional issues in depth as a signal that he or she may not have a healthy understanding of the boundary between coaching and therapy. Additionally, coaches who allow themselves to become personally involved in your life are most likely not maintaining the ethics of professional boundaries, either out of a lack of training or a lack of having done their own healing work.

Coaching should primarily be concerned with actualizing your goals through the concrete support tools of problem solving, structuring strategies, and accountability supports. Coaching has, by definition, a behavioral focus and is not therapy. I find that coaching is particularly effective at times in tandem with therapy (done by separate professionals) or after completing a phase of therapeutic work (and, therefore, may be done by the same therapist). Getting down to the brass tacks of actualizing your goals is no small challenge, and coaches can be highly effective support people.

Books and tapes, television, radio, and the internet resources

As we discussed in chapter five, self-help books, tapes, and the media or Internet are remarkable advantages that we have in our day and age for coping with problems. These tools not only allow us a private mechanism for beginning to understand and acknowledge our problems, but also steer us towards resources and people that can be the important next step in our healing journey. For the references named in this book, see the bibliography.

BIBLIOGRAPHY

A Shining Affliction: A Story of Harm and Healing in Psychotherapy, Annie G. Rogers, Ph.D., 1995, Viking Penguin.

Codependent No More: How to Stop Controlling Others and Start Caring for Yourself, Melody Beattie, 1987, Harper/Hazelden.

The Dance of Anger: A Woman's Guide to Changing the Patterns of Intimate Relationships, Harriet Lerner, Ph.D., 1985, Harper & Roy Publishers, Inc.

Diagnostic and Statistical Manual of Mental Disorders – Fourth Edition, DSM-IV, 1997, American Psychiatric Association.

Diagnostic and Statistical Manual of Mental Disorders – Third Edition, DSM-III, 1994, American Psychiatric Association.

Difficult Conversations: How to Discuss What Matters Most, Douglas Stone, Bruce Patton, Sheila Heen, Roger Fisher, 2000, Penguin USA.

The Drama of the Gifted Child: The Search for the True Self, Alice Miller, Revised edition, 1997, Basic Books – Division of Harper Collins Publishers, Inc.

For Your Own Good: Hidden Cruelty in Child-Rearing and the Roots of Violence, Alice Miller, Third Edition, 1990, The Noonday Press.

Getting the Love You Want: A Guide for Couples, Harville Hendrix, Ph.D., 2001, Owl Books.

People of the Lie: The Hope for Healing Human Evil, Scott Peck, M.D., 1985, Simon and Schuster.

Prep-Fighting for Your Marriage: Powerful Techniques for Handling Conflicts, Tape set, Markman, Stanley, & Blumberg, Ph.D.s, Denver, Colorado.

The Self Seekers, Richard Restak, M.D., 1982, Doubleday.

Where to Draw the Line: How to Set Healthy Boundaries Every Day, Anne Katherine, M.A., 2000, Simon & Schuster.

ABOUT THE AUTHOR

Eleanor Payson is a licensed marital and family therapist, practicing individual and marital therapy for the past eighteen years. Graduating from the University of Michigan in 1983 with her Masters in Social Work, she has continued her education on issues ranging from; chemical dependency and codependency, adult children of alcoholics, narcissistic and borderline personality disorders, relationship therapy, and attention deficit/hyperactivity disorder.

In 1993, Eleanor trained with Harville Hendrix, Ph.D., to become a certified imago therapist. Dr. Hendrix developed the concepts, techniques, and skills of imago therapy, outlining them in his book, *Getting the Love You Want: A Guide for Couples*. Helping couples achieve more rewarding and fulfilling relationships is one of Eleanor's greatest passions and goals. She has conducted numerous workshops teaching couples conflict resolution skills and the beginning concepts of imago therapy.

Since 1997, Eleanor has increasingly specialized in the unique and challenging difficulties that adults with attention deficit/hyperactivity disorder face. A national presenter at CHADD (Children and Adults with Attention Deficit/Hyperactivity Disorder) and ADDA (Adults with Attention Deficit/Hyperactivity Disorder) conferences, Eleanor addresses the many facets of coping in a relationship when one or both partners have AD/HD.

Eleanor's commitment to treating issues relating to narcissistic wounding over the past twenty years has led her to help people in codependent relationships with narcissistic individuals and inspired her determination to write her book.

She lives in Michigan with her husband, son, and three dogs. You can visit her on her web site at www.eleanorpayson.com, or email her for information regarding seminars, presentations, or consultations. See her web site to obtain her most current email address.